中华人民共和国

2018年国民经济和社会发展统计公报

STATISTICAL COMMUNIQUÉ OF THE PEOPLE'S REPUBLIC OF CHINA ON THE 2018 NATIONAL ECONOMIC AND SOCIAL DEVELOPMENT

国 家 统 计 局
National Bureau of Statistics of China

2019年2月28日
February 28, 2019

中国统计出版社
China Statistics Press

图书在版编目（CIP）数据

中华人民共和国2018年国民经济和社会发展统计公报 = Statistical Communiqué of the People's Republic of China on the 2018 National Economic and Social Development : 汉英对照 / 国家统计局编 . -- 北京 : 中国统计出版社 , 2019.3

ISBN 978-7-5037-8790-4

Ⅰ . ①中… Ⅱ . ①国… Ⅲ . ①国民经济发展－统计资料－公报－中国－ 2018 －汉、英②社会发展－统计资料－公报－中国－ 2018 －汉、英 Ⅳ . ① F124-66

中国版本图书馆 CIP 数据核字 (2019) 第 031240 号

中华人民共和国2018年国民经济和社会发展统计公报

作　　者 / 国家统计局
责任编辑 / 郭 栋
装帧设计 / 黄 晨
出版发行 / 中国统计出版社
地　　址 / 北京市丰台区西三环南路甲 6 号　　邮政编码 /100073
网　　址 /http://www.zgtjcbs.com
电　　话 /（010）63376866　63376907（发行部）
印　　刷 / 北京画中画印刷有限公司
经　　销 / 新华书店
开　　本 /880×1230 毫米　1/16
字　　数 /92 千字
印　　张 /5
版　　别 /2019 年 3 月第 1 版
版　　次 /2019 年 3 月北京第 1 次印刷
定　　价 /38.00 元

目 录

CONTENTS

中华人民共和国
2018 年国民经济和社会发展统计公报[1]

国家统计局
2019 年 2 月 28 日

2018 年，面对复杂严峻的国际环境和艰巨繁重的改革发展稳定任务，在以习近平同志为核心的党中央坚强领导下，各地区各部门以习近平新时代中国特色社会主义思想为指导，全面贯彻党的十九大和十九届二中、三中全会精神，按照党中央、国务院决策部署，统筹推进“五位一体”总体布局，协调推进“四个全面”战略布局，坚持稳中求进工作总基调，深入贯彻新发展理念，落实高质量发展要求，以供给侧结构性改革为主线，着力深化改革扩大开放，坚决打好防范化解重大风险、精准脱贫、污染防治三大攻坚战，有效应对外部环境深刻变化，统筹稳增长、促改革、调结构、惠民生、防风险，做好稳就业、稳金融、稳外贸、稳外资、稳投资、稳预期工作，经济运行总体平稳、稳中有进，质量效益稳步提升，人民生活持续改善，保持了经济持续健康发展和社会大局稳定，朝着实现全面建成小康社会的目标迈出了新的步伐。

[1] 本公报中数据均为初步统计数。各项统计数据均未包括香港特别行政区、澳门特别行政区和台湾省。部分数据因四舍五入的原因，存在总计与分项合计不等的情况。

一、综合

初步核算，全年国内生产总值[2]900309 亿元，比上年增长 6.6%。其中，第一产业增加值 64734 亿元，增长 3.5%；第二产业增加值 366001 亿元，增长 5.8%；第三产业增加值 469575 亿元，增长 7.6%。第一产业增加值占国内生产总值的比重为 7.2%，第二产业增加值比重为 40.7%，第三产业增加值比重为 52.2%。全年最终消费支出对国内生产总值增长的贡献率为 76.2%，资本形成总额的贡献率为 32.4%，货物和服务净出口的贡献率为 −8.6%。人均国内生产总值 64644 元，比上年增长 6.1%。国民总收入[3]896915 亿元，比上年增长 6.5%。全国万元国内生产总值能耗[4]比上年下降 3.1%。全员劳动生产率[5]为 107327 元／人，比上年提高 6.6%。

图 1　2014–2018 年国内生产总值及其增长速度

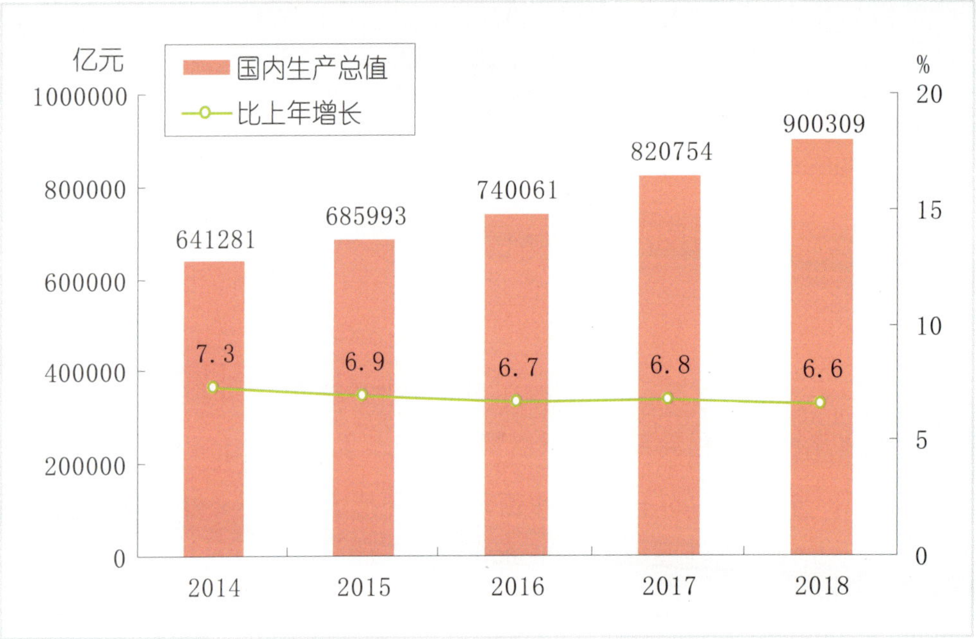

[2] 国内生产总值、各产业增加值、人均国内生产总值和国民总收入绝对数按现价计算，增长速度按不变价格计算。根据第三次全国农业普查结果，对国内生产总值、三次产业增加值比重、全员劳动生产率等历史数据进行了修订。

[3] 国民总收入，原称国民生产总值，是指一个国家或地区所有常住单位在一定时期内所获得的初次分配收入总额，等于国内生产总值加上来自国外的初次分配收入净额。

[4] 万元国内生产总值能耗按 2015 年价格计算。

[5] 全员劳动生产率为国内生产总值（按 2015 年价格计算）与全部就业人员的比率。

图 2　2014–2018 年三次产业增加值占国内生产总值比重

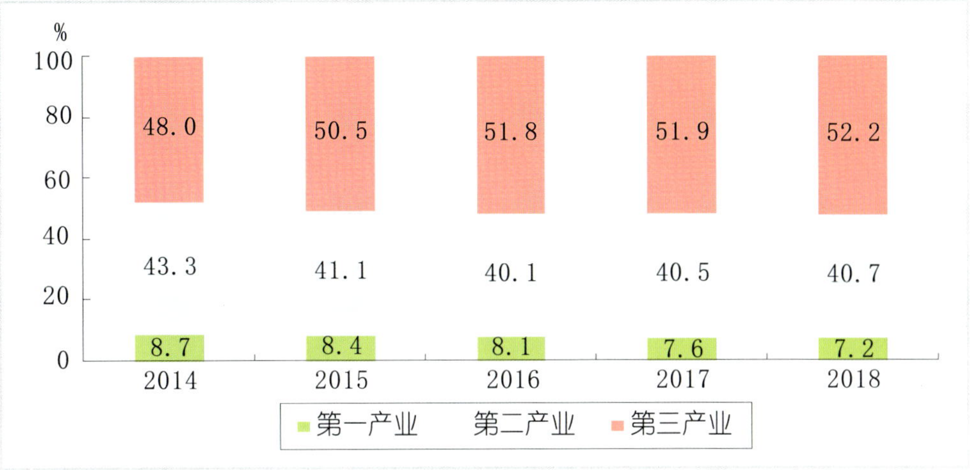

图 3　2014–2018 年万元国内生产总值能耗降低率

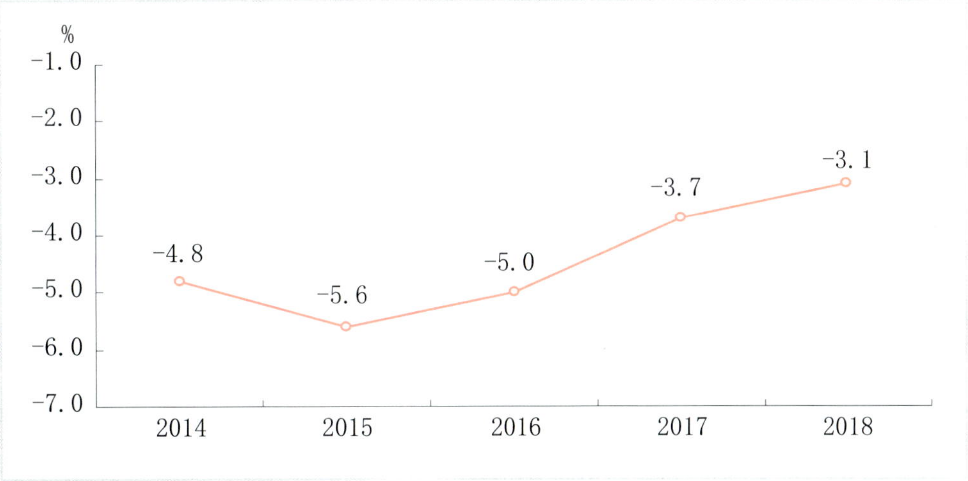

图 4　2014–2018 年全员劳动生产率

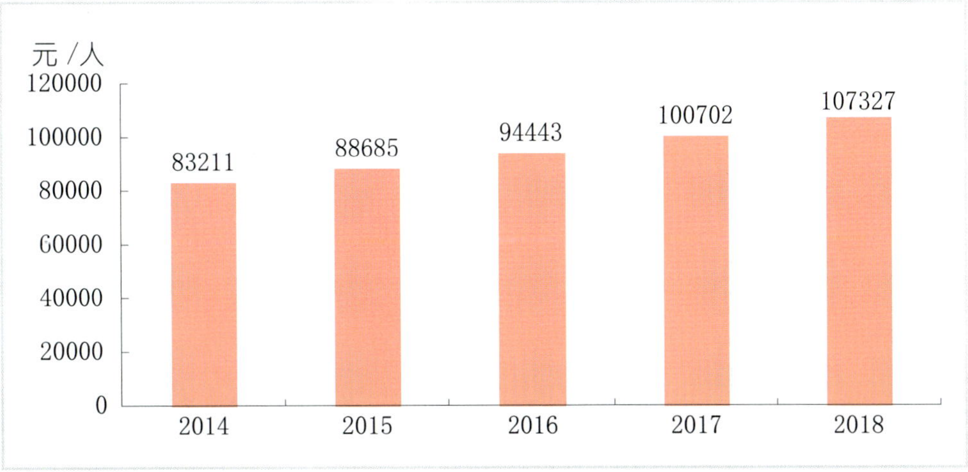

年末全国大陆总人口139538万人，比上年末增加530万人，其中城镇常住人口83137万人，占总人口比重（常住人口城镇化率）为59.58%，比上年末提高1.06个百分点。户籍人口城镇化率为43.37%，比上年末提高1.02个百分点。全年出生人口1523万人，出生率为10.94‰；死亡人口993万人，死亡率为7.13‰；自然增长率为3.81‰。全国人户分离的人口[6]2.86亿人，其中流动人口[7]2.41亿人。

表1　2018年年末人口数及其构成

指　标	年末数（万人）	比重（%）
全国总人口	139538	100.0
其中：城镇	83137	59.58
乡村	56401	40.42
其中：男性	71351	51.1
女性	68187	48.9
其中：0-15岁（含不满16周岁）[8]	24860	17.8
16-59岁（含不满60周岁）	89729	64.3
60周岁及以上	24949	17.9
其中：65周岁及以上	16658	11.9

年末全国就业人员77586万人，其中城镇就业人员43419万人。全年城镇新增就业1361万人，比上年增加10万人。年末全国城镇调查失业率为4.9%，比上年末下降0.1个百分点；城镇登记失业率为3.8%，下降0.1个百分点。全国农民工[9]总量28836万人，比上年增长0.6%。其中，外出农民工17266万人，增长0.5%；本地农民工11570万人，增长0.9%。

[6]人户分离的人口是指居住地与户口登记地所在的乡镇街道不一致且离开户口登记地半年及以上的人口。

[7]流动人口是指人户分离人口中扣除市辖区内人户分离的人口。市辖区内人户分离的人口是指一个直辖市或地级市所辖区内和区与区之间，居住地和户口登记地不在同一乡镇街道的人口。

[8] 2018年年末，0—14岁（含不满15周岁）人口为23523万人，15—59岁（含不满60周岁）人口为91066万人。

[9]年度农民工数量包括年内在本乡镇以外从业6个月及以上的外出农民工和在本乡镇内从事非农产业6个月及以上的本地农民工两部分。

图 5 2014—2018 年城镇新增就业人数

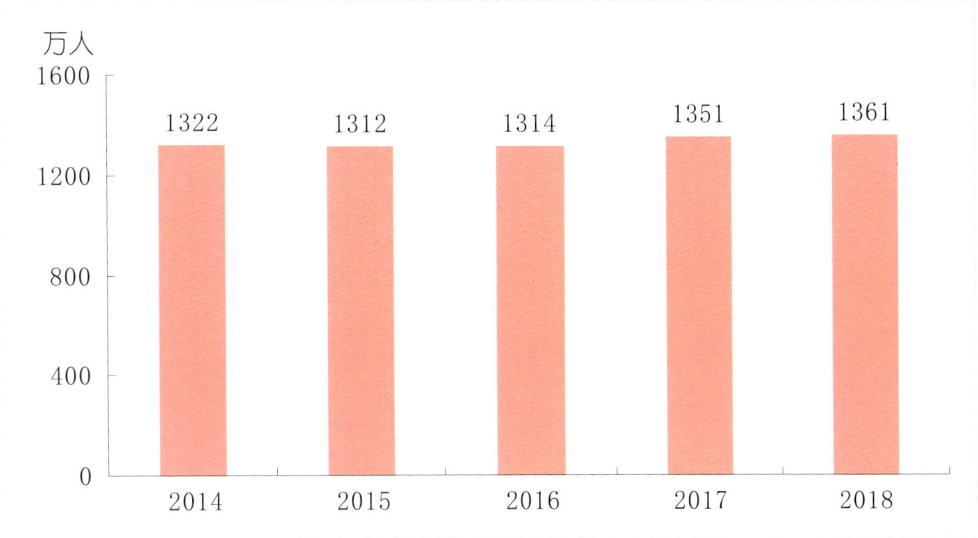

全年居民消费价格比上年上涨 2.1%。工业生产者出厂价格上涨 3.5%。工业生产者购进价格上涨 4.1%。固定资产投资价格上涨 5.4%。农产品生产者价格[10]下降 0.9%。12 月份 70 个大中城市新建商品住宅销售价格月同比上涨的城市个数为 69 个，下降的为 1 个。

图 6 2018 年居民消费价格月度涨跌幅度

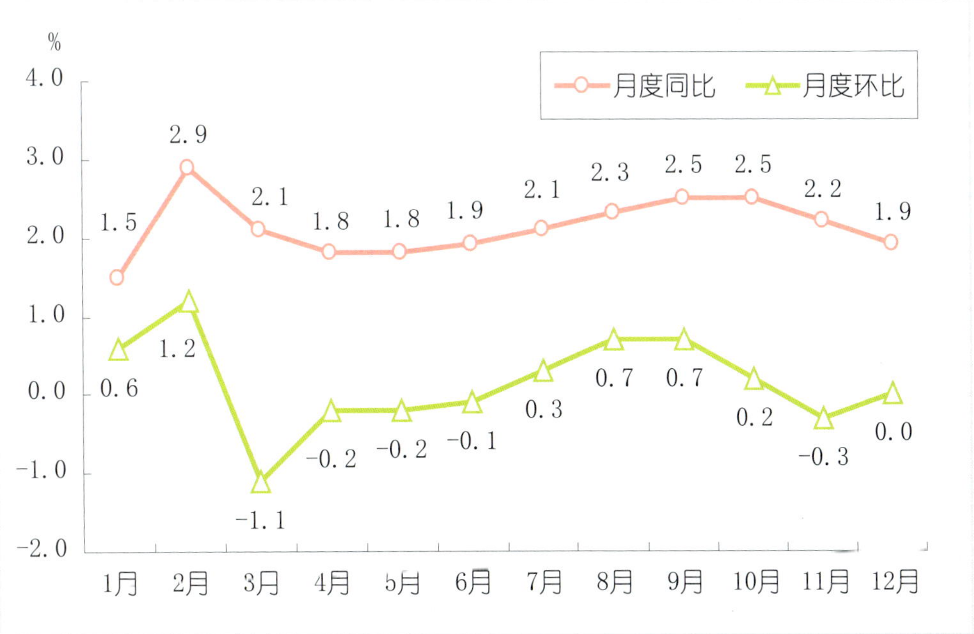

[10] 农产品生产者价格是指农产品生产者直接出售其产品时的价格。

表2　2018年居民消费价格比上年涨跌幅度

单位：%

指　标	全　国	城　市	农　村
居民消费价格	2.1	2.1	2.1
其中：食品烟酒	1.9	2.1	1.1
衣　着	1.2	1.1	1.5
居　住[11]	2.4	2.1	3.3
生活用品及服务	1.6	1.6	1.6
交通和通信	1.7	1.6	1.8
教育文化和娱乐	2.2	2.3	2.2
医疗保健	4.3	4.6	3.7
其他用品和服务	1.2	1.2	1.2

年末国家外汇储备30727亿美元，比上年末减少672亿美元。全年人民币平均汇率为1美元兑6.6174元人民币，比上年升值2.0%。

图7　2014—2018年年末国家外汇储备

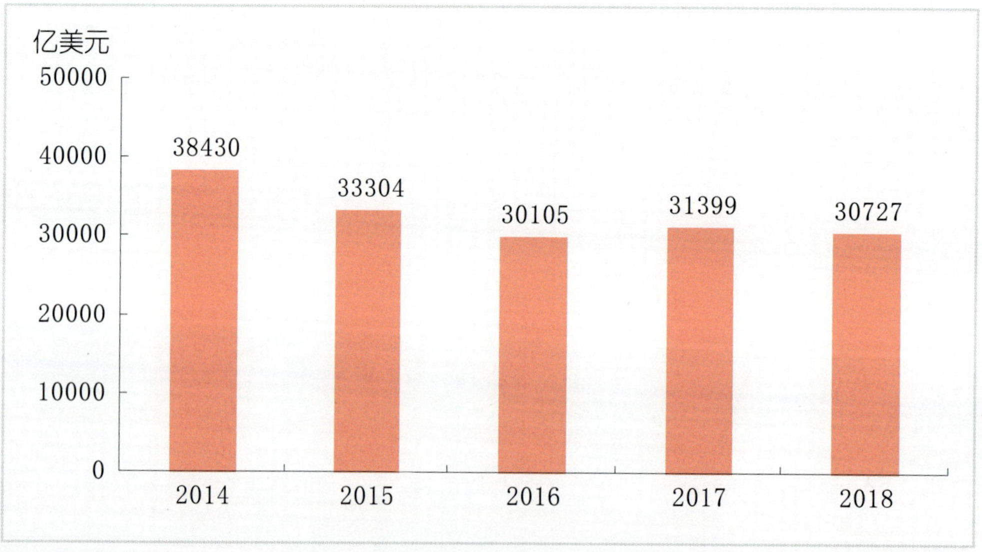

[11] 居住类价格包括租赁房房租、住房保养维修及管理、水电燃料等价格。

供给侧结构性改革深入推进。全年全国工业产能利用率[12]为 76.5%。其中，煤炭开采和洗选业产能利用率为 70.6%，比上年提高 2.4 个百分点；黑色金属冶炼和压延加工业产能利用率为 78.0%，提高 2.2 个百分点。年末商品房待售面积 52414 万平方米，比上年末减少 6510 万平方米。其中，商品住宅待售面积 25091 万平方米，减少 5072 万平方米。年末规模以上工业企业资产负债率为 56.5%，比上年末下降 0.5 个百分点[13]。全年规模以上工业企业每百元主营业务收入中的成本为 83.88 元，比上年下降 0.20 元。全年生态保护和环境治理业、农业固定资产投资（不含农户）分别比上年增长 43.0% 和 15.4%。

新动能持续发展壮大。全年规模以上工业中，战略性新兴产业[14]增加值比上年增长 8.9%。高技术制造业[15]增加值增长 11.7%，占规模以上工业增加值的比重为 13.9%。装备制造业[16]增加值增长 8.1%，占规模以上工业增加值的比重为 32.9%。全年规模以上服务业[17]中，战略性新兴服务业[18]营业收入比上年增长 14.6%。全年高技术产业投资[19]比上年增长 14.9%，工业技术改造投资[20]增长 12.8%。全年新能源汽车产量 115 万辆，比上年增长 66.2%；智能电视产量 11376 万台，增长 17.7%。全年网上零售额[21]90065 亿元，比上年增长 23.9%。

脱贫攻坚成效显著。按照每人每年 2300 元（2010 年不变价）的农村贫困标准计算，年末农村贫困人口 1660 万人，比上年末减少 1386 万人[22]；贫困发生率[23]1.7%，比上年下降 1.4 个百分点。

[12] 产能利用率是指实际产出与生产能力（均以价值量计量）的比率。企业的实际产出是指企业报告期内的工业总产值；企业的生产能力是指报告期内，在劳动力、原材料、燃料、运输等保证供给的情况下，生产设备（机械）保持正常运行，企业可实现的、并能长期维持的产品产出。

[13] 由于统计制度规定的口径调整、统计执法、剔除重复数据、企业改革剥离等因素，2018 年规模以上工业企业财务指标增速及变化按可比口径计算。

[14] 工业战略性新兴产业包括节能环保产业，新一代信息技术产业，生物产业，高端装备制造产业，新能源产业，新材料产业，新能源汽车产业等七大产业中的工业相关行业。

[15] 高技术制造业包括医药制造业，航空、航天器及设备制造业，电子及通信设备制造业，计算机及办公设备制造业，医疗仪器设备及仪器仪表制造业，信息化学品制造业。

[16] 装备制造业包括金属制品业，通用设备制造业，专用设备制造业，汽车制造业，铁路、船舶、航空航天和其他运输设备制造业，电气机械和器材制造业，计算机、通信和其他电子设备制造业，仪器仪表制造业。

[17] 规模以上服务业统计范围包括年营业收入 1000 万元及以上，或年末从业人员 50 人及以上的交通运输、仓储和邮政业，信息传输、软件和信息技术服务业，房地产业（不含房地产开发经营），租赁和商务服务业，科学研究和技术服务业，水利、环境和公共设施管理业，教育，卫生和社会工作；年营业收入 500 万元及以上，或年末从业人员 50 人及以上的居民服务、修理和其他服务业，文化、体育和娱乐业法人单位。

[18] 战略性新兴服务业包括节能环保产业，新一代信息技术产业，生物产业，高端装备制造产业，新能源产业，新材料产业，新能源汽车产业等七大产业中的服务业相关行业。

[19] 高技术产业投资包括医药制造、航空航天器及设备制造等六大类高技术制造业投资和信息服务、电子商务服务等九大类高技术服务业投资。

[20] 工业技术改造投资是指工业企业利用新技术、新工艺、新设备、新材料对现有设施、工艺条件及生产服务等进行改造提升，实现内涵式发展的投资活动。

[21] 网上零售额是指通过公共网络交易平台（主要从事实物商品交易的网上平台，包括自建网站和第三方平台）实现的商品和服务零售额。2018 年网上零售额增速按可比口径计算。

[22] 减贫人口等于当年贫困人口减去上年贫困人口，也相当于当年脱贫人口减去当年返贫人口。

[23] 贫困发生率是指贫困人口占目标调查人口的比重。

全年贫困地区[24]农村居民人均可支配收入10371元，比上年增长10.6%，扣除价格因素，实际增长8.3%。

图8 2014—2018年年末全国农村贫困人口和贫困发生率

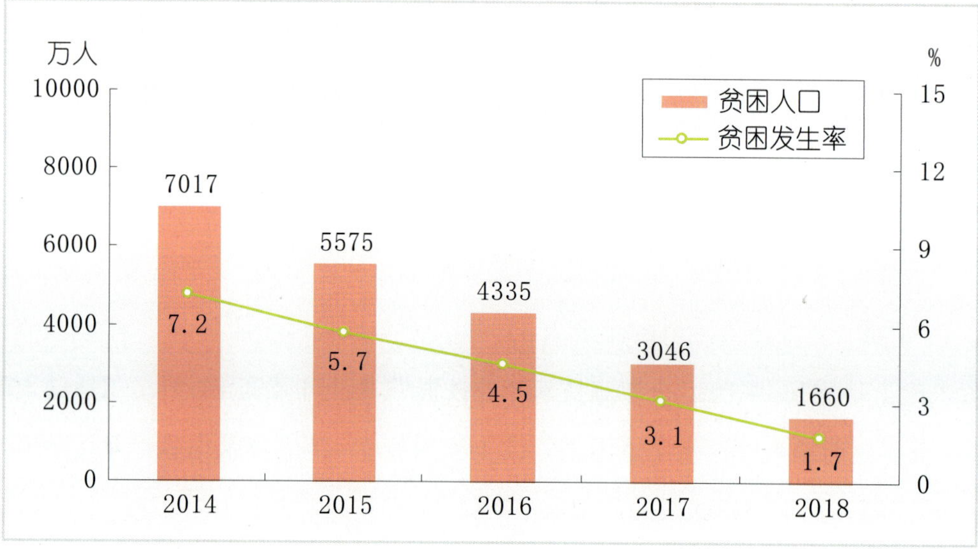

二、农业[25]

全年粮食种植面积11704万公顷，比上年减少95万公顷。其中，小麦种植面积2427万公顷，减少24万公顷；稻谷种植面积3019万公顷，减少56万公顷；玉米种植面积4213万公顷，减少27万公顷。棉花种植面积335万公顷，增加16万公顷。油料种植面积1289万公顷，减少33万公顷。糖料种植面积163万公顷，增加9万公顷。

全年粮食产量65789万吨，比上年减少371万吨，减产0.6%。其中，夏粮产量13878万吨，减产2.1%；早稻产量2859万吨，减产4.3%；秋粮产量49052万吨，增产0.1%。全年谷物产量61019万吨，比上年减产0.8%。其中，稻谷产量21213万吨，减产0.3%；小麦产量13143万吨，减产2.2%；玉米产量25733万吨，减产0.7%。

[24] 贫困地区包括集中连片特困地区和片区外的国家扶贫开发工作重点县，原共有832个县。2017年开始将新疆阿克苏地区纳入贫困监测范围。

[25] 农、牧、渔业等历史数据根据第三次全国农业普查结果进行了修订。

图 9　2014–2018 年粮食产量

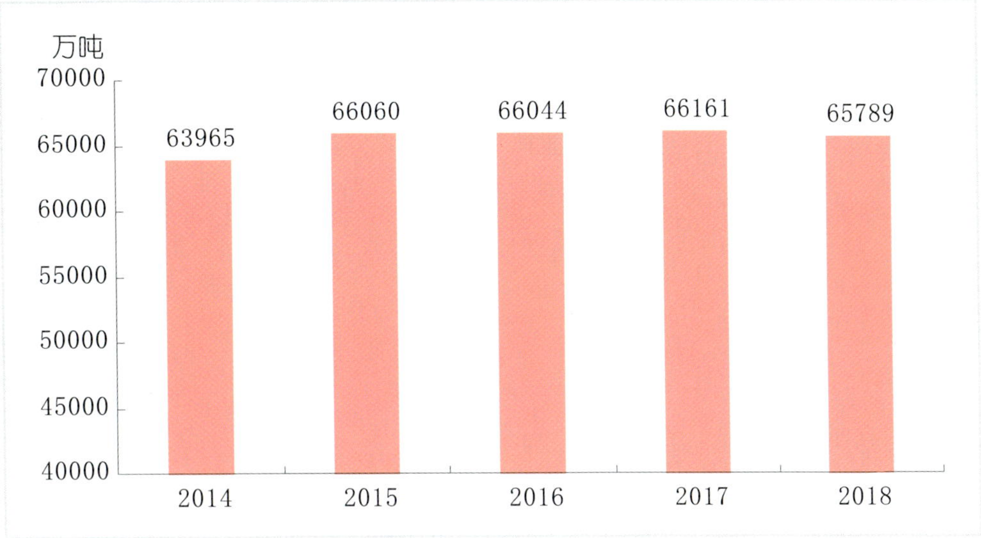

全年棉花产量 610 万吨，比上年增产 7.8%。油料产量 3439 万吨，减产 1.0%。糖料产量 11976 万吨，增产 5.3%。茶叶产量 261 万吨，增产 5.9%。

全年猪牛羊禽肉产量 8517 万吨，比上年下降 0.3%。其中，猪肉产量 5404 万吨，下降 0.9%；牛肉产量 644 万吨，增长 1.5%；羊肉产量 475 万吨，增长 0.8%；禽肉产量 1994 万吨，增长 0.6%。禽蛋产量 3128 万吨，增长 1.0%。牛奶产量 3075 万吨，增长 1.2%。年末生猪存栏 42817 万头，下降 3.0%；生猪出栏 69382 万头，下降 1.2%。

全年水产品产量 6469 万吨，比上年增长 0.4%。其中，养殖水产品产量 5018 万吨，增长 2.3%；捕捞水产品产量 1451 万吨，下降 5.7%。

全年木材产量 8432 万立方米，比上年增长 0.4%。

全年新增耕地灌溉面积 72 万公顷，新增高效节水灌溉面积 144 万公顷。

三、工业和建筑业

全年全部工业增加值 305160 亿元，比上年增长 6.1%。规模以上工业增加值增长 6.2%。在规模以上工业中，分经济类型看，国有控股企业增加值增长 6.2%；股份制企业增长 6.6%，外商及港澳台商投资企业增长 4.8%；私营企业增长 6.2%。分门类看，采矿业增长 2.3%，制造业增长 6.5%，电力、热力、燃气及水生产和供应业增长 9.9%。

图 10　2014—2018 年全部工业增加值及其增长速度

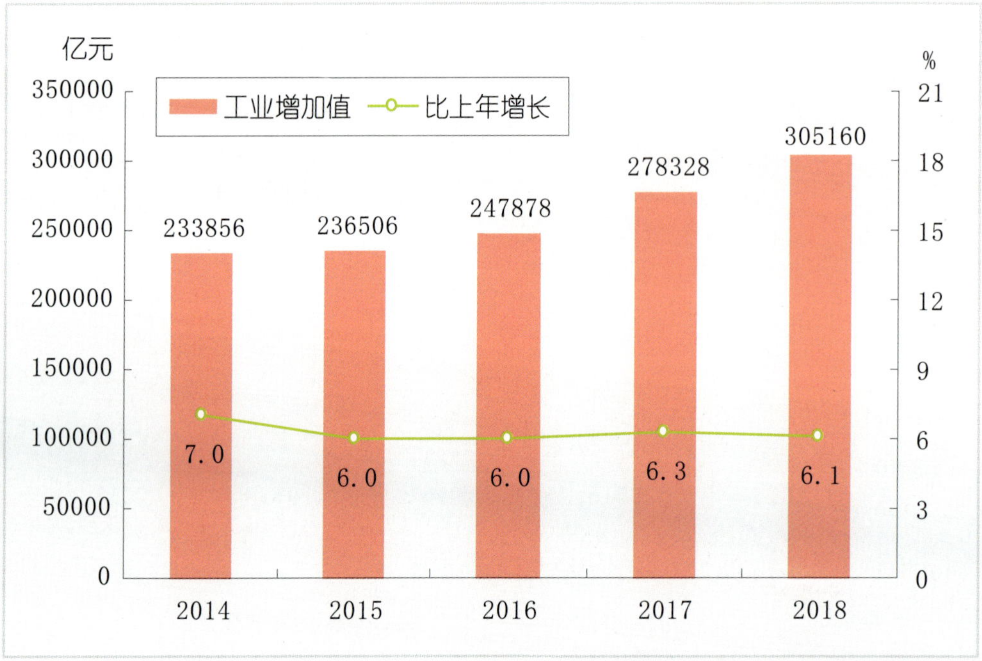

全年规模以上工业中，农副食品加工业增加值比上年增长5.9%，纺织业增长1.0%，化学原料和化学制品制造业增长3.6%，非金属矿物制品业增长4.6%，黑色金属冶炼和压延加工业增长7.0%，通用设备制造业增长7.2%，专用设备制造业增长10.9%，汽车制造业增长4.9%，电气机械和器材制造业增长7.3%，计算机、通信和其他电子设备制造业增长13.1%，电力、热力生产和供应业增长9.6%。

表3 2018年主要工业产品产量及其增长速度[26]

产品名称	单 位	产 量	比上年增长（%）
纱	万吨	2958.9	-7.3
布	亿米	657.3	-4.9
化学纤维	万吨	5011.1	2.7
成品糖	万吨	1524.1	3.5
卷烟	亿支	23358.7	-0.4
彩色电视机	万台	18834.8	18.2
其中：液晶电视机	万台	18825.2	19.5
家用电冰箱	万台	7993.2	-3.9
房间空气调节器	万台	20486.0	14.7
一次能源生产总量	亿吨标准煤	37.7	5.0
原煤	亿吨	36.8	4.5
原油	万吨	18910.6	-1.3
天然气	亿立方米	1602.7	8.3
发电量	亿千瓦小时	71117.7	7.7
其中：火电[27]	亿千瓦小时	50738.6	6.7
水电	亿千瓦小时	12342.3	3.0
核电	亿千瓦小时	2943.6	18.7
粗钢	万吨	92800.9	6.6
钢材[28]	万吨	110551.7	5.6
十种有色金属	万吨	5702.7	3.7
其中：精炼铜（电解铜）	万吨	902.9	0.7
原 铝（电解铝）	万吨	3580.2	7.5
水泥	亿吨	22.1	-5.3
硫酸（折100%）	万吨	9129.8	-0.9
烧碱（折100%）	万吨	3420.2	2.7
乙烯	万吨	1841.0	1.1
化肥（折100%）	万吨	5424.4	-7.9
发电机组（发电设备）	万千瓦	10600.5	-10.3
汽车	万辆	2781.9	-4.1
其中：基本型乘用车（轿车）	万辆	1160.1	-2.9
运动型多用途乘用车（SUV）	万辆	927.4	-7.7
大中型拖拉机	万台	24.3	-29.3
集成电路	亿块	1739.5	11.2
程控交换机	万线	1006.6	7.3
移动通信手持机	万台	179846.4	-4.8
微型计算机设备	万台	30700.2	0.1
工业机器人	万台（套）	14.8	6.4

[26] 2017年部分产品产量数据进行了核实调整，2018年产量增速按调整后的可比口径计算。

[27] 火电包括燃煤发电量，燃油发电量，燃气发电量，余热、余压、余气发电量，垃圾焚烧发电量，生物质发电量。

[28] 钢材产量数据中含企业之间重复加工钢材约21800万吨。

年末全国发电装机容量189967万千瓦，比上年末增长6.5%[29]。其中[30]，火电装机容量114367万千瓦，增长3.0%；水电装机容量35226万千瓦，增长2.5%；核电装机容量4466万千瓦，增长24.7%；并网风电装机容量18426万千瓦，增长12.4%；并网太阳能发电装机容量17463万千瓦，增长33.9%。

全年规模以上工业企业利润66351亿元，比上年增长10.3%[31]。分经济类型看，国有控股企业利润18583亿元，比上年增长12.6%；股份制企业46975亿元，增长14.4%，外商及港澳台商投资企业16776亿元，增长1.9%；私营企业17137亿元，增长11.9%。分门类看，采矿业利润5246亿元，比上年增长40.1%；制造业56964亿元，增长8.7%；电力、热力、燃气及水生产和供应业4141亿元，增长4.3%。全年规模以上工业企业主营业务收入利润率为6.49%，比上年提高0.11个百分点。

全年全社会建筑业增加值61808亿元，比上年增长4.5%。全国具有资质等级的总承包和专业承包建筑业企业利润8104亿元，比上年增长8.2%，其中国有控股企业2470亿元，增长8.5%。

图11 2014—2018年建筑业增加值及其增长速度

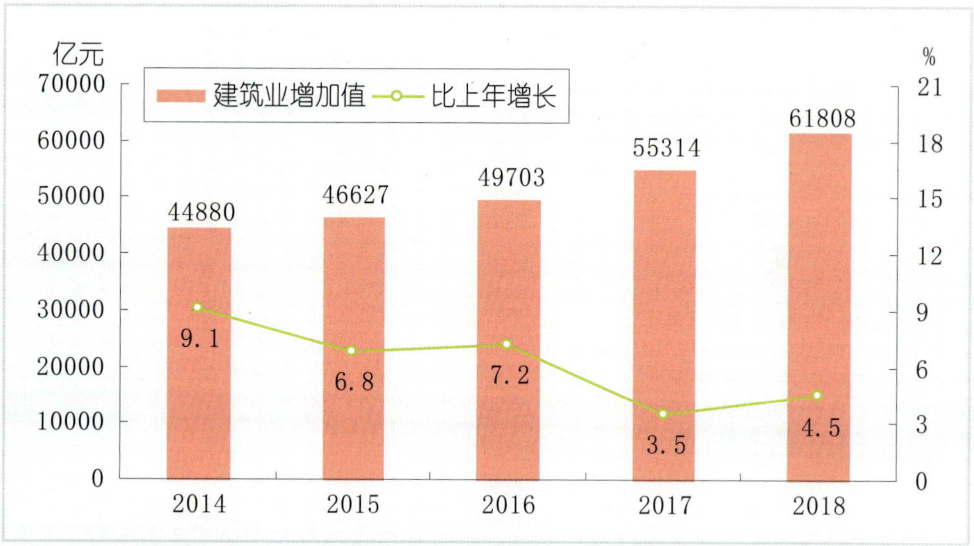

四、服务业

全年批发和零售业增加值84201亿元，比上年增长6.2%；交通运输、仓储和邮政业增加值40550亿元，增长8.1%；住宿和餐饮业增加值16023亿元，增长6.5%；金融业增加值69100亿元，增长4.4%；房地产业增加值59846亿元，增长3.8%；信息传输、软件和信息技术服务业增加值

[29] 2018年，中国电力企业联合会对发电装机容量统计范围进行了调整，增速按可比口径计算。
[30] 少量发电装机容量（如地热等）公报中未列出。
[31] 见注释[13]。

32431 亿元，增长 30.7%；租赁和商务服务业增加值 24427 亿元，增长 8.9%。全年规模以上服务业企业营业收入比上年增长 11.4%，营业利润增长 6.5%。

图 12　2014—2018 年服务业增加值及其增长速度

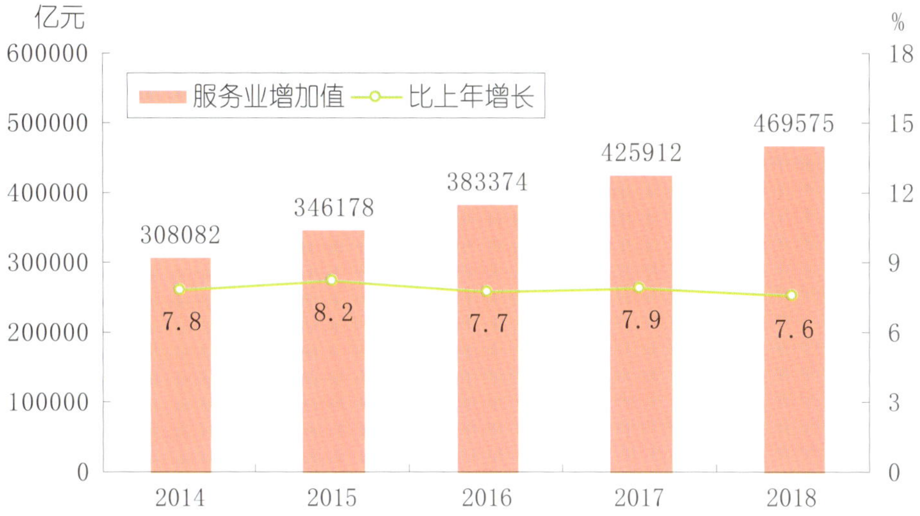

全年货物运输总量 515 亿吨，比上年增长 7.1%。货物运输周转量 205452 亿吨公里，增长 4.1%。全年规模以上港口完成货物吞吐量 133 亿吨，比上年增长 2.7%[32]，其中外贸货物吞吐量 42 亿吨，增长 2.0%。规模以上港口集装箱吞吐量 24955 万标准箱，增长 5.2%。

表 4　2018 年各种运输方式完成货物运输量及其增长速度

指　标	单　位	绝对数	比上年增长（%）
货物运输总量	**亿吨**	**514.6**	**7.1**
铁　路	亿吨	40.3	9.2
公　路	亿吨	395.9	7.4
水　运	亿吨	69.9	4.7
民　航	万吨	738.5	4.6
管　道	亿吨	8.5	5.4
货物运输周转量	**亿吨公里**	**205451.6**	**4.1**
铁　路	亿吨公里	28821.0	6.9
公　路	亿吨公里	71202.5	6.6
水　运	亿吨公里	99303.6	0.7
民　航	亿吨公里	262.4	7.7
管　道	亿吨公里	5862.0	22.5

[32] 2018 年部分规模以上港口货物吞吐量统计范围进行调整，扩大至全港企业，相关指标增速按可比口径计算。

全年旅客运输总量179亿人次，比上年下降3.1%[33]。旅客运输周转量34213亿人公里，增长4.3%。

表5　2018年各种运输方式完成旅客运输量及其增长速度

指　标	单　位	绝对数	比上年增长（%）
旅客运输总量	**亿人次**	**179.2**	**-3.1**
铁　路	亿人次	33.7	9.4
公　路	亿人次	136.5	-6.3
水　运	亿人次	2.8	-0.5
民　航	亿人次	6.1	10.9
旅客运输周转量	**亿人公里**	**34213.5**	**4.3**
铁　路	亿人公里	14146.6	5.1
公　路	亿人公里	9275.5	-5.0
水　运	亿人公里	79.8	2.7
民　航	亿人公里	10711.6	12.6

年末全国民用汽车保有量24028万辆（包括三轮汽车和低速货车906万辆），比上年末增长10.5%，其中私人汽车保有量20730万辆，增长10.9%。民用轿车保有量13451万辆，增长10.4%，其中私人轿车12589万辆，增长10.3%。

全年完成邮政行业业务总量[34]12345亿元，比上年增长26.4%。邮政业全年完成邮政函件业务26.8亿件，包裹业务0.2亿件，快递业务量507.1亿件，快递业务收入6038亿元。全年完成电信业务总量[35]65556亿元，比上年增长137.9%。电信业新增移动电话交换机容量[36]17267万户，达到259453万户。年末全国电话用户总数174835万户，其中移动电话用户156610万户。移动电话普及率上升至112.2部/百人。固定互联网宽带接入用户[37]40738万户，比上年末增加5884万户，其中固定互联网光纤宽带接入用户[38]36833万户，增加7440万户；移动宽带用户[39]130565万户，增加17413万户。全年移动互联网用户接入流量711亿GB，比上年增长189.1%。全年软件和信息技术服务业[40]完成软件业务收入63061亿元，按可比口径计算，比上年增长14.2%。

[33]旅客运输总量包括铁路、公路、水运、民航营业性旅客运输量，其中公路旅客运输量占70%以上。近年来，随着人们出行方式的变化，居民自驾出行、网络约车及拼车人数增长较快，分流了公路客运量，导致旅客运输总量下降。

[34]邮政行业业务总量按2010年价格计算。

[35]电信业务总量按2015年价格计算。

[36]移动电话交换机容量是指移动电话交换机根据一定话务模型和交换机处理能力计算出来的最大同时服务用户的数量。

[37]固定互联网宽带接入用户是指报告期末在电信企业登记注册，通过xDSL、FTTx+LAN、FTTH/O以及其他宽带接入方式和普通专线接入公众互联网的用户。

[38]固定互联网光纤宽带接入用户是指报告期末在电信企业登记注册，通过FTTH或FTTO方式接入公众互联网的用户。

[39]移动宽带用户是指报告期末在计费系统拥有使用信息，占用3G或4G网络资源的在网用户。

[40]软件和信息技术服务业包括软件开发，集成电路设计，信息系统集成和物联网技术服务，运行维护服务，信息处理和存储支持服务，信息技术咨询服务，数字内容服务和其他信息技术服务等行业。

图 13　2014—2018 年快递业务量及其增长速度

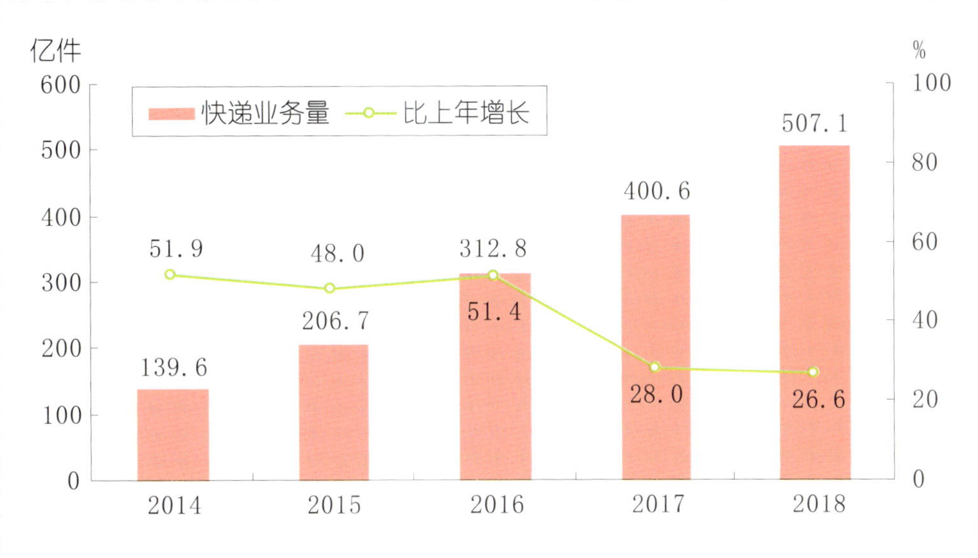

图 14　2014—2018 年年末固定互联网宽带接入用户数和移动宽带用户数

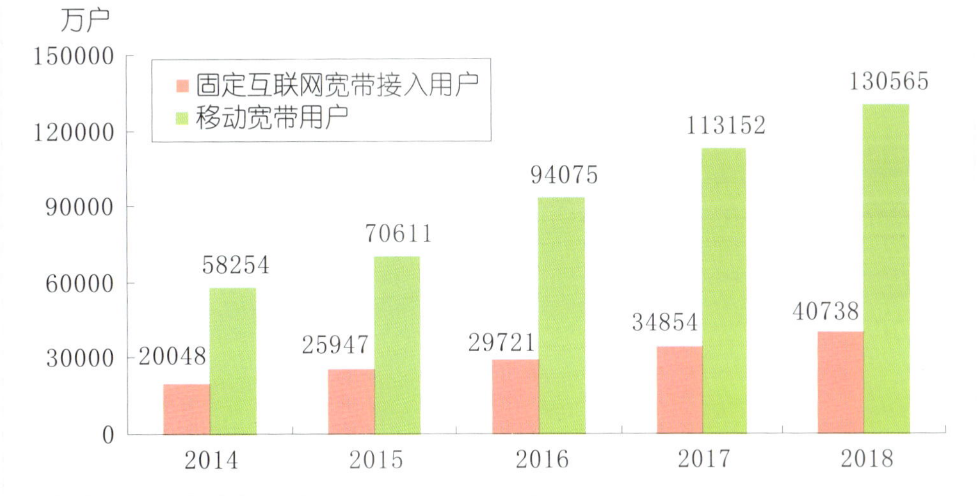

五、国内贸易[41]

全年社会消费品零售总额 380987 亿元，比上年增长 9.0%。按经营地统计，城镇消费品零售额 325637 亿元，增长 8.8%；乡村消费品零售额 55350 亿元，增长 10.1%。按消费类型统计，商品零售额 338271 亿元，增长 8.9%；餐饮收入额 42716 亿元，增长 9.5%。

在限额以上单位商品零售额中，粮油、食品类零售额比上年增长 10.2%，饮料类增长 9.0%，

[41] 根据第三次全国农业普查结果及有关制度规定，对 2017 年社会消费品零售总额及分项基数进行修订，2018 年增速按可比口径计算。

烟酒类增长7.4%，服装、鞋帽、针纺织品类增长8.0%，化妆品类增长9.6%，金银珠宝类增长7.4%，日用品类增长13.7%，家用电器和音像器材类增长8.9%，中西药品类增长9.4%，文化办公用品类增长3.0%，家具类增长10.1%，通讯器材类增长7.1%，建筑及装潢材料类增长8.1%，石油及制品类增长13.3%，汽车类下降2.4%。

全年实物商品网上零售额70198亿元，比上年增长25.4%，占社会消费品零售总额的比重为18.4%，比上年提高3.4个百分点。

六、固定资产投资[42]

全年全社会固定资产投资645675亿元，比上年增长5.9%。其中固定资产投资（不含农户）635636亿元，增长5.9%。分区域看[43]，东部地区投资比上年增长5.7%，中部地区投资增长10.0%，西部地区投资增长4.7%，东北地区投资增长1.0%。

在固定资产投资（不含农户）中，第一产业投资22413亿元，比上年增长12.9%；第二产业投资237899亿元，增长6.2%；第三产业投资375324亿元，增长5.5%。民间固定资产投资[44]394051

图15　2014-2018年三次产业投资占固定资产投资（不含农户）比重

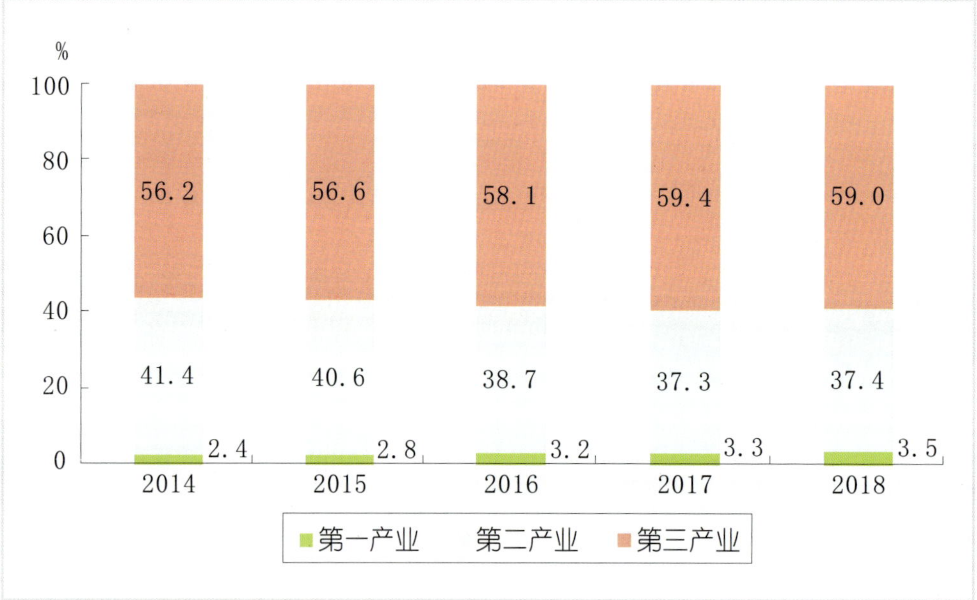

[42]根据统计执法检查和第四次全国经济普查单位清查结果，对2017年固定资产投资基数进行一些修订，2018年增速按可比口径计算。

[43]东部地区是指北京、天津、河北、上海、江苏、浙江、福建、山东、广东和海南10省（市）；中部地区是指山西、安徽、江西、河南、湖北和湖南6省；西部地区是指内蒙古、广西、重庆、四川、贵州、云南、西藏、陕西、甘肃、青海、宁夏和新疆12省（区、市）；东北地区是指辽宁、吉林和黑龙江3省。

[44]民间固定资产投资是指具有集体、私营、个人性质的内资企事业单位以及由其控股（包括绝对控股和相对控股）的企业单位建造或购置固定资产的投资。

亿元，增长 8.7%，占固定资产投资（不含农户）的比重为 62.0%。基础设施投资[45]增长 3.8%。六大高耗能行业投资增长 1.4%。

表 6　2018 年分行业固定资产投资（不含农户）增长速度

行　业	比上年增长（%）	行　业	比上年增长（%）
总　计	5.9	金融业	-13.1
农、林、牧、渔业	12.3	房地产业[46]	8.3
采矿业	4.1	租赁和商务服务业	14.2
制造业	9.5	科学研究和技术服务业	13.6
电力、热力、燃气及水生产和供应业	-6.7	水利、环境和公共设施管理业	3.3
建筑业	-13.9	居民服务、修理和其他服务业	-14.4
批发和零售业	-21.5	教育	7.2
交通运输、仓储和邮政业	3.9	卫生和社会工作	8.4
住宿和餐饮业	-3.4	文化、体育和娱乐业	21.2
信息传输、软件和信息技术服务业	4.0	公共管理、社会保障和社会组织	-18.0

表 7　2018 年固定资产投资新增主要生产与运营能力

指　标	单　位	绝对数
新增 220 千伏及以上变电设备	万千伏安	22082
新建铁路投产里程	公里	4683
其中：高速铁路[47]	公里	4100
增、新建铁路复线投产里程	公里	4711
电气化铁路投产里程	公里	6474
新改建公路里程	公里	356045
其中：高速公路	公里	6063
港口万吨级码头泊位新增通过能力	万吨 / 年	26428
新增民用运输机场	个	6
新增光缆线路长度	万公里	578

[45] 基础设施投资包括交通运输、邮政业，电信、广播电视和卫星传输服务业，互联网和相关服务业，水利、环境和公共设施管理业投资。

[46] 房地产业投资除房地产开发投资外，还包括建设单位自建房屋以及物业管理、中介服务和其他房地产投资。

[47] 高速铁路是指线路最大速度 200 公里 / 小时及以上的铁路和 200 公里 / 小时以下仅运行动车组列车的铁路。

全年房地产开发投资120264亿元，比上年增长9.5%。其中住宅投资85192亿元，增长13.4%；办公楼投资5996亿元，下降11.3%；商业营业用房投资14177亿元，下降9.4%。

全年全国棚户区住房改造开工626万套，基本建成511万套。全国农村地区建档立卡贫困户危房改造157万户[48]。

表8 2018年房地产开发和销售主要指标及其增长速度

指　标	单　位	绝对数	比上年增长(%)
投资额	亿元	120264	9.5
其中：住宅	亿元	85192	13.4
房屋施工面积	万平方米	822300	5.2
其中：住宅	万平方米	569987	6.3
房屋新开工面积	万平方米	209342	17.2
其中：住宅	万平方米	153353	19.7
房屋竣工面积	万平方米	93550	-7.8
其中：住宅	万平方米	66016	-8.1
商品房销售面积	万平方米	171654	1.3
其中：住宅	万平方米	147929	2.2
本年到位资金	亿元	165963	6.4
其中：国内贷款	亿元	24005	-4.9
个人按揭贷款	亿元	23706	-0.8

七、对外经济

全年货物进出口总额305050亿元，比上年增长9.7%。其中，出口164177亿元，增长7.1%；进口140874亿元，增长12.9%。货物进出口顺差23303亿元，比上年减少5217亿元。对“一带一路”[49]沿线国家进出口总额83657亿元，比上年增长13.3%。其中，出口46478亿元，增长7.9%；进口37179亿元，增长20.9%。

[48]各省（自治区、直辖市）汇总上报截至2018年12月底建档立卡贫困户农村危房改造实际竣工数。
[49]“一带一路”是指“丝绸之路经济带”和“21世纪海上丝绸之路”。

图 16 2014—2018 年货物进出口总额

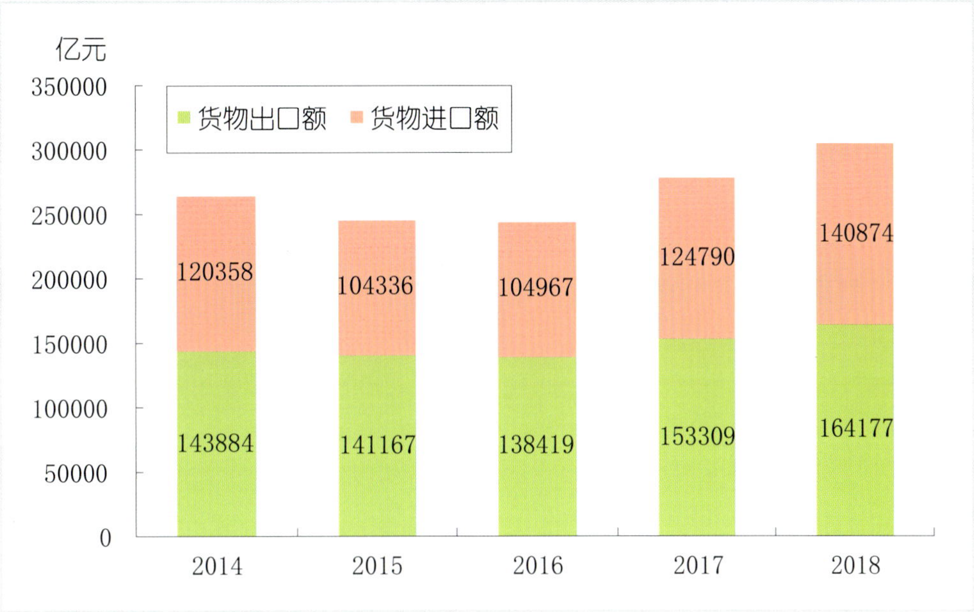

表 9 2018 年货物进出口总额及其增长速度

指 标	金额（亿元）	比上年增长（%）
货物进出口总额	305050	9.7
货物出口额	164177	7.1
其中：一般贸易	92405	10.9
加工贸易	52676	2.5
其中：机电产品	96457	7.9
高新技术产品	49374	9.3
货物进口额	140874	12.9
其中：一般贸易	83947	14.3
加工贸易	31097	6.6
其中：机电产品	63727	10.3
高新技术产品	44340	12.2
货物进出口顺差	23303	—

表 10　2018 年主要商品出口数量、金额及其增长速度

商品名称	单　位	数　量	比上年增长（%）	金　额（亿元）	比上年增长（%）
钢材	万吨	6934	-8.1	3984	7.7
纺织纱线、织物及制品	—	—	—	7851	5.1
服装及衣着附件	—	—	—	10413	-2.3
鞋类	万吨	448	-0.4	3095	-5.4
家具及其零件	—	—	—	3544	4.8
箱包及类似容器	万吨	316	2.0	1787	-1.0
玩具	—	—	—	1662	2.3
塑料制品	万吨	1312	12.3	2870	9.3
集成电路	亿个	2171	6.2	5591	23.5
自动数据处理设备及其部件	万台	147296	-4.4	11355	6.0
手持或车载无线电话机	万台	111918	-7.8	9343	9.8
集装箱	万个	340	13.5	685	20.9
液晶显示板	万个	175810	-9.3	1527	-12.5
汽车	万辆	115	11.3	972	8.3

表 11　2018 年主要商品进口数量、金额及其增长速度

商品名称	单　位	数　量	比上年增长（%）	金　额（亿元）	比上年增长（%）
谷物及谷物粉	万吨	2047	-20.0	385	-12.4
大豆	万吨	8803	-7.9	2502	-6.9
食用植物油	万吨	629	9.0	313	2.0
铁矿砂及其精矿	万吨	106447	-1.0	4984	-4.0
煤及褐煤	万吨	28123	3.9	1613	4.9
原油	万吨	46190	10.1	15882	43.1
成品油	万吨	3348	13.0	1333	35.6
天然气	万吨	9039	31.9	2552	62.1
初级形状的塑料	万吨	3284	14.5	3718	13.2
纸浆	万吨	2479	4.5	1300	25.1
钢材	万吨	1317	-1.0	1083	5.5
未锻轧铜及铜材	万吨	530	12.9	2469	16.5
集成电路	亿个	4176	10.8	20584	16.9
汽车	万辆	113	-8.5	3331	-2.7

表12 2018年对主要国家和地区货物进出口金额、增长速度及其比重

国家和地区	出口额（亿元）	比上年增长（%）	占全部出口比重（%）	进口额（亿元）	比上年增长（%）	占全部进口比重（%）
欧盟	26974	7.0	16.4	18067	9.2	12.8
美国	31603	8.6	19.2	10195	-2.3	7.2
东盟	21066	11.3	12.8	17722	11.0	12.6
日本	9709	4.4	5.9	11906	6.2	8.5
韩国	7174	3.1	4.4	13495	12.3	9.6
中国香港	19966	5.7	12.2	564	13.8	0.4
中国台湾	3212	7.9	2.0	11714	11.0	8.3
巴西	2214	12.9	1.3	5119	28.2	3.6
俄罗斯	3167	9.1	1.9	3909	39.4	2.8
印度	5054	9.5	3.1	1242	12.2	0.9
南非	1072	6.9	0.7	1799	8.9	1.3

全年服务进出口[50]总额52402亿元，比上年增长11.5%。其中，服务出口17658亿元，增长14.6%；服务进口34744亿元，增长10.0%。服务进出口逆差17086亿元。

全年外商直接投资（不含银行、证券、保险领域）新设立企业60533家，比上年增长69.8%。实际使用外商直接投资金额8856亿元，增长0.9%，折1350亿美元，增长3.0%。其中“一带一路”沿线国家对华直接投资新设立企业4479家，增长16.1%；对华直接投资金额424亿元，增长13.2%，折64亿美元，增长16.0%。全年高技术制造业实际使用外资898亿元，增长35.1%，折137亿美元，增长38.1%。

表13 2018年外商直接投资（不含银行、证券、保险领域）及其增长速度

行　业	企业数（家）	比上年增长（%）	实际使用金额（亿元）	比上年增长（%）
总　计	60533	69.8	8856	0.9
其中：农、林、牧、渔业	741	5.0	53	-26.4
制造业	6152	23.4	2713	20.1
电力、热力、燃气及水生产和供应业	284	-23.7	291	23.6
交通运输、仓储和邮政业	754	45.8	314	-16.0
信息传输、软件和信息技术服务业	7222	127.9	773	-44.4
批发和零售业	22853	86.1	643	-16.5
房地产业	1053	42.9	1489	31.4
租赁和商务服务业	9099	78.9	1196	6.4
居民服务、修理和其他服务业	485	39.0	37	-2.6

[50]服务进出口按照《国际收支手册（第六版）》标准统计，增速按可比口径计算。

全年对外非金融类直接投资额7974亿元，比上年下降1.6%，折1205亿美元，增长0.3%。其中，对“一带一路”沿线国家非金融类直接投资额156亿美元，增长8.9%。

表14 2018年对外非金融类直接投资额及其增长速度

行 业	金额（亿美元）	比上年增长（%）
总 计	1205	0.3
其中：农、林、牧、渔业	18	-20.3
采矿业	92	11.3
制造业	188	-1.6
电力、热力、燃气及水生产和供应业	32	-0.9
建筑业	74	0.8
批发和零售业	106	-57.5
交通运输、仓储和邮政业	58	92.7
信息传输、软件和信息技术服务业	68	-33.7
房地产业	40	82.0
租赁和商务服务业	446	27.6

全年对外承包工程完成营业额11186亿元，比上年下降1.7%，折1690亿美元，增长0.3%。其中，对“一带一路”沿线国家完成营业额893亿美元，增长4.4%，占对外承包工程完成营业额比重为52.8%。对外劳务合作派出各类劳务人员49万人。

八、财政金融

全年全国一般公共预算收入183352亿元，比上年增长6.2%。其中税收收入156401亿元，比上年增加12031亿元，增长8.3%。全年各地共发行地方政府置换债券13130亿元，平均发行利率约3.89%。2015-2018年，置换债券累计发行12.2万亿元，基本完成既定的存量政府债务置换目标。经过置换，年末地方政府债务平均利率比2014年末降低约6.5个百分点，累计节约利息约1.7万亿元。

图 17 2014–2018 年全国一般公共预算收入

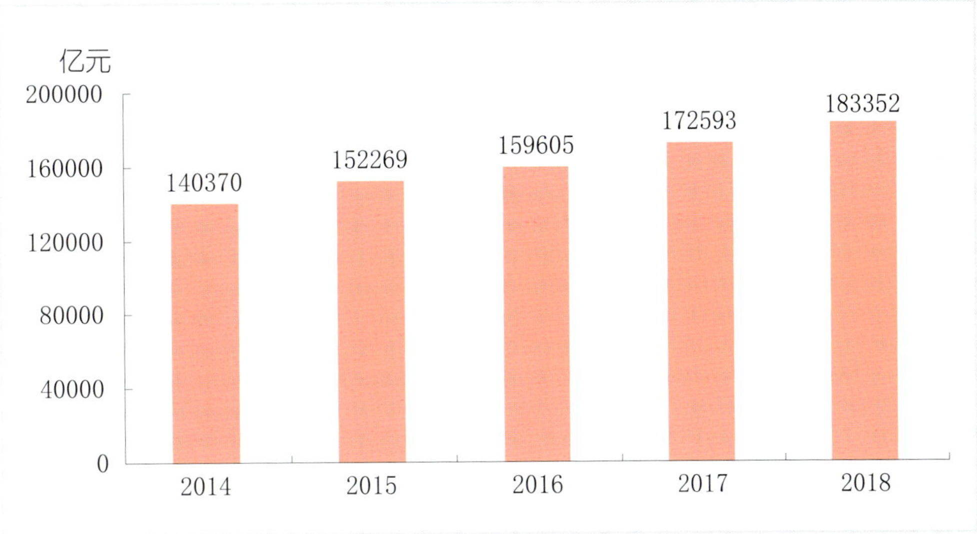

注：图中 2014 年至 2017 年数据为全国一般公共预算收入决算数，2018 年为执行数。

年末广义货币供应量（M_2）余额 182.7 万亿元，比上年末增长 8.1%；狭义货币供应量（M_1）余额 55.2 万亿元，增长 1.5%；流通中货币（M_0）余额 7.3 万亿元，增长 3.6%。

全年社会融资规模增量[51]19.3 万亿元，按可比口径计算，比上年少 3.1 万亿元；年末社会融资规模存量[52]200.7 万亿元，比上年末增长 9.8%。年末全部金融机构本外币各项存款余额 182.5 万亿元，比年初增加 13.2 万亿元，其中人民币各项存款余额 177.5 万亿元，增加 13.4 万亿元。全部金融机构本外币各项贷款余额 141.8 万亿元，增加 16.2 万亿元，其中人民币各项贷款余额 136.3 万亿元，增加 16.2 万亿元。

表 15 2018 年年末全部金融机构本外币存贷款余额及其增长速度

指 标	年末数（亿元）	比上年末增长（%）
各项存款	**1825158**	**7.8**
其中：境内住户存款	724439	11.1
其中：人民币	716038	11.2
境内非金融企业存款	589105	3.1
各项贷款	**1417516**	**12.9**
其中：境内短期贷款	443200	7.8
境内中长期贷款	854571	13.8

[51] 社会融资规模增量是指一定时期内实体经济从金融体系获得的资金总额。
[52] 社会融资规模存量是指一定时期末（月末、季末或年末）实体经济从金融体系获得的资金余额。

年末主要农村金融机构（农村信用社、农村合作银行、农村商业银行）人民币贷款余额169822亿元，比年初增加20002亿元。全部金融机构人民币消费贷款余额377903亿元，增加62709亿元。其中，个人短期消费贷款余额87994亿元，增加19989亿元；个人中长期消费贷款余额289909亿元，增加42720亿元。

全年境内交易场所累计筹资[53]64365亿元，比上年增加13572亿元。其中，首次公开发行A股105只，筹资1378亿元，减少923亿元；A股现金再融资（包括公开增发、定向增发、配股、优先股）5505亿元，减少2504亿元；各类主体通过沪深交易所发行债券（包括公司债、可转债、可交换债、政策性金融债、地方政府债和企业资产支持证券）筹资56878亿元，增加17731亿元；全国中小企业股份转让系统[54]新增挂牌公司577家，挂牌公司累计筹资604亿元。

全年发行公司信用类债券[55]7.79万亿元，比上年增加1.92万亿元。

全年保险公司原保险保费收入[56]38017亿元，比上年增长3.9%。其中，寿险业务原保险保费收入20723亿元，健康险和意外伤害险业务原保险保费收入6524亿元，财产险业务原保险保费收入10770亿元。支付各类赔款及给付12298亿元。其中，寿险业务给付4389亿元，健康险和意外伤害险业务赔款及给付2012亿元，财产险业务赔款5897亿元。

九、居民收入消费和社会保障

全年全国居民人均可支配收入28228元，比上年增长8.7%，扣除价格因素，实际增长6.5%。全国居民人均可支配收入中位数[57]24336元，增长8.6%。按常住地分，城镇居民人均可支配收入39251元，比上年增长7.8%，扣除价格因素，实际增长5.6%。城镇居民人均可支配收入中位数36413元，增长7.6%。农村居民人均可支配收入14617元，比上年增长8.8%，扣除价格因素，实际增长6.6%。农村居民人均可支配收入中位数13066元，增长9.2%。按全国居民五等份收入分组[58]，低收入组人均可支配收入6440元，中间偏下收入组人均可支配收入14361元，中间收入组人均可支配收入23189元，中间偏上收入组人均可支配收入36471元，高收入组人均可支配收入70640元。全国农民工人均月收入3721元，比上年增长6.8%。

[53]境内股票市场筹资额按上市日统计。

[54]全国中小企业股份转让系统又称“新三板”，是2012年经国务院批准设立的全国性证券交易场所。全年全国中小企业股份转让系统挂牌公司累计筹资不含优先股。

[55]公司信用类债券包括非金融企业债务融资工具、企业债券以及公司债、可转债等。

[56]原保险保费收入是指保险企业确认的原保险合同保费收入。

[57]人均收入中位数是指将所有调查户按人均收入水平从低到高（或从高到低）顺序排列，处于最中间位置调查户的人均收入。

[58]全国居民五等份收入分组是指将所有调查户按人均收入水平从高到低顺序排列，平均分为五个等份，处于最高20%的收入群体为高收入组，依此类推依次为中间偏上收入组、中间收入组、中间偏下收入组、低收入组。

全年全国居民人均消费支出 19853 元，比上年增长 8.4%，扣除价格因素，实际增长 6.2%。按常住地分，城镇居民人均消费支出 26112 元，增长 6.8%，扣除价格因素，实际增长 4.6%；农村居民人均消费支出 12124 元，增长 10.7%，扣除价格因素，实际增长 8.4%。全国居民恩格尔系数为 28.4%，比上年下降 0.9 个百分点，其中城镇为 27.7%，农村为 30.1%。

图 18　2014–2018 年全国居民人均可支配收入及其增长速度

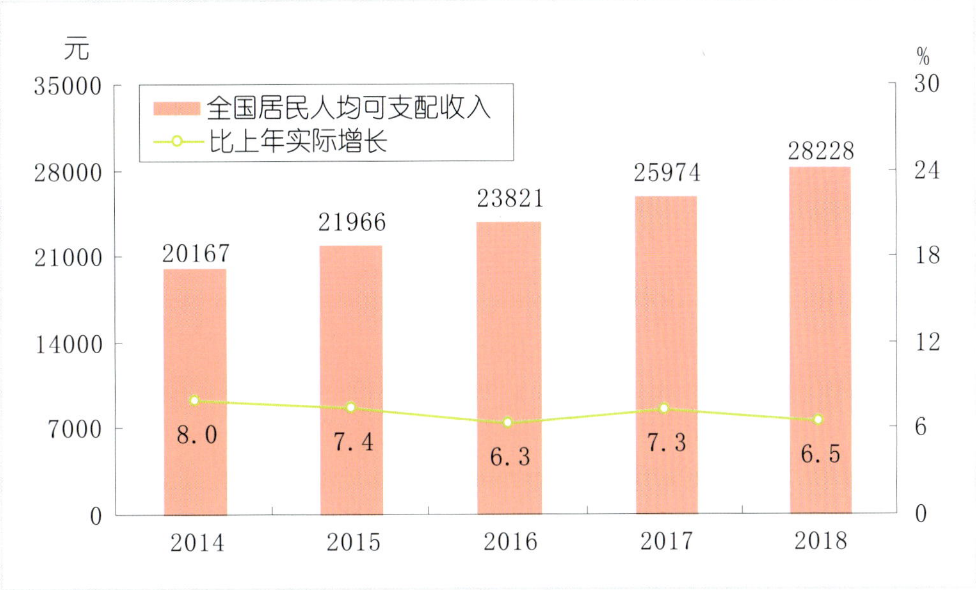

图 19　2018 年全国居民人均消费支出及其构成

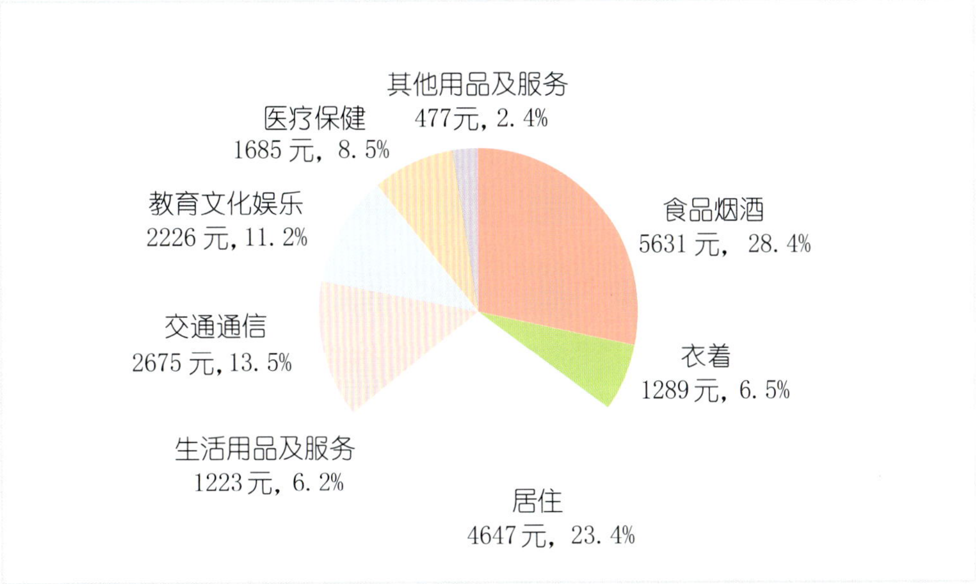

年末全国参加城镇职工基本养老保险人数41848万人，比上年末增加1555万人。参加城乡居民基本养老保险人数52392万人，增加1137万人。参加基本医疗保险人数134452万人，增加16771万人。其中，参加职工基本医疗保险人数31673万人，增加1351万人；参加城乡居民基本医疗保险人数89741万人，增加2382万人。参加失业保险人数19643万人，增加859万人。年末全国领取失业保险金人数223万人。参加工伤保险人数23868万人，增加1145万人，其中参加工伤保险的农民工8085万人，增加278万人。参加生育保险人数20435万人，增加1135万人。年末全国共有1008万人享受城市居民最低生活保障，3520万人享受农村居民最低生活保障，455万人享受农村特困人员[59]救助供养，全年临时救助[60]1075万人次。全年资助4972万人参加基本医疗保险，医疗救助3825万人次。国家抚恤、补助退役军人和其他优抚对象861万人。

年末全国共有各类提供住宿的社会服务机构3.3万个，其中养老服务机构3.0万个，儿童服务机构664个。社会服务床位[61]782.4万张，其中养老服务床位746.3万张，儿童服务床位10.4万张。年末共有社区服务中心2.7万个，社区服务站14.5万个。

十、科学技术和教育

全年研究与试验发展（R&D）经费支出19657亿元，比上年增长11.6%，与国内生产总值之比为2.18%，其中基础研究经费1118亿元。全年国家重点研发计划共安排1052个项目，国家科技重大专项共安排563个课题，国家自然科学基金共资助44504个项目。截至年底，正在运行的国家重点实验室501个，累计建设国家工程研究中心132个，国家工程实验室217个，国家企业技术中心1480家。国家科技成果转化引导基金累计设立21支子基金，资金总规模313亿元。全年境内外专利申请432.3万件，比上年增长16.9%；授予专利权244.7万件，增长33.3%；PCT专利申请受理量[62]为5.5万件。截至年底，有效专利838.1万件，其中境内有效发明专利160.2万件，每万人口发明专利拥有量11.5件。全年共签订技术合同41.2万项，技术合同成交金额17697亿元，比上年增长31.8%。

---

[59] 农村特困人员是指无劳动能力，无生活来源，无法定赡养、抚养、扶养义务人或者其法定义务人无履行义务能力的农村老年人、残疾人以及未满16周岁的未成年人。

[60] 临时救助是国家对遭遇突发事件、意外伤害、重大疾病或其他特殊原因导致基本生活陷入困境，其他社会救助制度暂时无法覆盖或救助之后基本生活暂时仍有严重困难的家庭或个人给予的应急性、过渡性的救助。

[61] 社会服务床位数除收养性机构外，还包括救助类机构、社区类机构以及军休所、军供站等机构的床位。

[62] PCT专利申请受理量是指国家知识产权局作为PCT专利申请受理局受理的PCT专利申请数量。PCT(Patent Cooperation Treaty)即专利合作条约，是专利领域的一项国际合作条约。

图 20 2014-2018 年研究与试验发展（R&D）经费支出及其增长速度

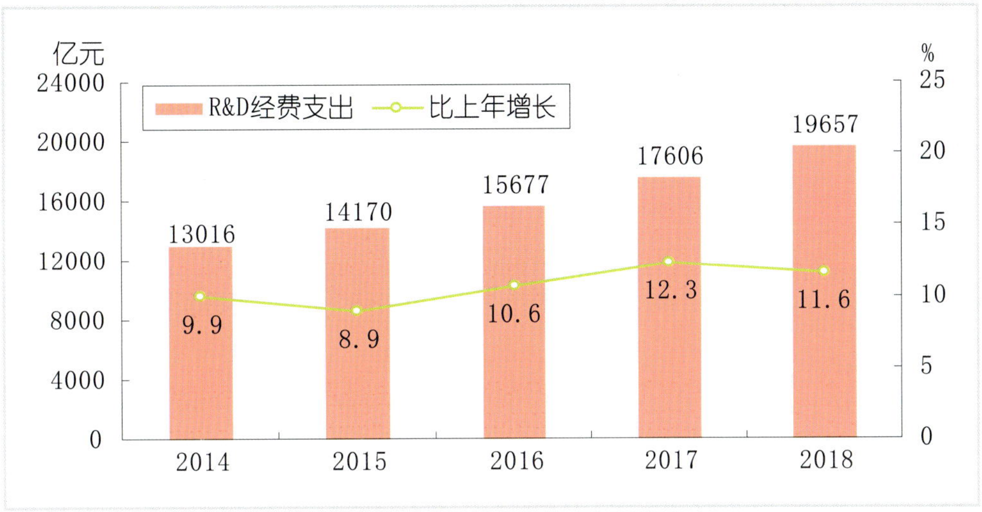

表 16 2018 年专利申请、授权和有效专利情况

指　标	专利数（万件）	比上年增长（%）
专利申请数	**432.3**	**16.9**
其中：境内专利申请	412.1	17.3
其中：发明专利申请	154.2	11.6
其中：境内发明专利	138.1	11.9
专利授权数	**244.7**	**33.3**
其中：境内专利授权	231.9	36.0
其中：发明专利授权	43.2	2.9
其中：境内发明专利	34.0	6.0
年末有效专利数	**838.1**	**17.3**
其中：境内有效专利	739.9	19.3
其中：有效发明专利	236.6	13.5
其中：境内有效发明专利	160.2	18.1

全年成功完成38次宇航发射。嫦娥四号探测器成功着陆月球背面并通过中继星将数据传回地球，标志着人类首次月球背面巡视探测任务正式开启；北斗三号基本系统完成建设，开始提供全球服务；我国地震立体观测体系首个天基平台中意电磁监测试验卫星、中法航天合作的首颗卫星中法海洋卫星成功发射。第二艘航母出海试航，国产大型水陆两栖飞机水上首飞，港珠澳大桥正式通车运营。

年末全国共有国家质检中心 791 家。全国现有产品质量、体系和服务认证机构 484 个，累计完成对 63 万家企业的认证。全国共有法定计量技术机构 5030 个，全年强制检定计量器具 10406 万台

（件）。全年制定、修订国家标准2668项，其中新制定1935项。全年制造业产品质量合格率[63]为93.93%。

全年研究生教育招生85.8万人，在学研究生273.1万人，毕业生60.4万人。普通本专科招生791.0万人，在校生2831.0万人，毕业生753.3万人。中等职业教育[64]招生557.0万人，在校生1555.2万人，毕业生487.3万人。普通高中招生792.7万人，在校生2375.4万人，毕业生779.2万人。初中招生1602.6万人，在校生4652.6万人，毕业生1367.8万人。普通小学招生1867.3万人，在校生10339.3万人，毕业生1616.5万人。特殊教育招生12.4万人，在校生66.6万人，毕业生8.1万人。学前教育在园幼儿4656.4万人。九年义务教育巩固率为94.2%，高中阶段毛入学率为88.8%。

图21　2014—2018年普通本专科、中等职业教育及普通高中招生人数

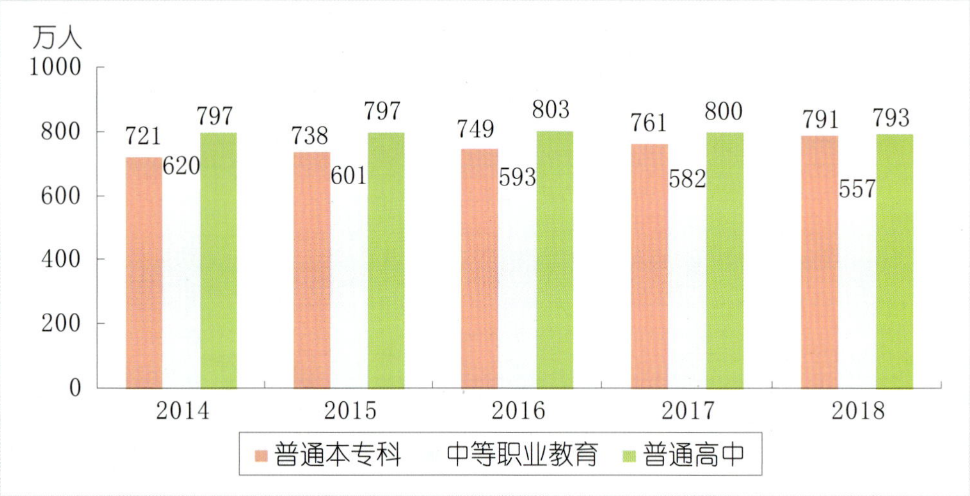

十一、文化旅游、卫生健康和体育

年末全国文化系统共有艺术表演团体2075个，博物馆3331个。全国共有公共图书馆3173个，总流通[65]84529万人次；文化馆3326个。有线电视实际用户2.14亿户，其中有线数字电视实际用户2.02亿户。年末广播节目综合人口覆盖率为98.9%，电视节目综合人口覆盖率为99.3%。全年生产电视剧323部13726集，电视动画片86257分钟。全年生产故事影片902部，科教、纪录、动

[63]制造业产品质量合格率是指以产品质量检验为手段，按照规定的方法、程序和标准实施质量抽样检测，判定为质量合格的样品数占全部抽样样品数的百分比，统计调查样本覆盖制造业的29个行业。

[64]中等职业教育包括普通中专、成人中专、职业高中和技工学校。

[65]总流通人次是指本年度内到图书馆场馆接受图书馆服务的总人次，包括借阅书刊、咨询问题以及参加各类读者活动等。

画和特种影片[66]180 部。出版各类报纸 340 亿份，各类期刊 24 亿册，图书 95 亿册（张），人均图书拥有量[67]6.85 册（张）。年末全国共有档案馆 4210 个，已开放各类档案 14016 万卷（件）。

全年国内游客 55.4 亿人次，比上年增长 10.8%；国内旅游收入 51278 亿元，增长 12.3%。入境游客 14120 万人次，增长 1.2%。其中，外国人 3054 万人次，增长 4.7%；香港、澳门和台湾同胞 11066 万人次，增长 0.3%。在入境游客中，过夜游客 6290 万人次，增长 3.6%。国际旅游收入 1271 亿美元，增长 3.0%。国内居民出境 16199 万人次，增长 13.5%。其中因私出境 15502 万人次，增长 14.1%；赴港澳台出境 9919 万人次，增长 14.0%。

图 22　2014—2018 年国内游客人次及其增长速度

年末全国共有医疗卫生机构 100.4 万个，其中医院 3.2 万个，在医院中有公立医院 1.2 万个，民营医院 2.0 万个；基层医疗卫生机构 95.0 万个，其中乡镇卫生院 3.6 万个，社区卫生服务中心（站）3.5 万个，门诊部（所）24.8 万个，村卫生室 63.0 万个；专业公共卫生机构 1.9 万个，其中疾病预防控制中心 3469 个，卫生监督所（中心）3141 个。年末卫生技术人员 950 万人，其中执业医师和执业助理医师 358 万人，注册护士 412 万人。医疗卫生机构床位 845 万张，其中医院 656 万张，乡镇卫生院 134 万张。全年总诊疗人次[68]84.2 亿人次，出院人数[69]2.6 亿人。

[66] 特种影片是指那些采用与常规影院放映在技术、设备、节目方面不同的电影展示方式，如巨幕电影、立体电影、立体特效（4D）电影、动感电影、球幕电影等。

[67] 人均图书拥有量是指在一年内全国平均每人能拥有的当年出版图书册数。

[68] 总诊疗人次指所有诊疗工作的总人次数，包括门诊、急诊、出诊、预约诊疗、单项健康检查、健康咨询指导（不含健康讲座）人次。

[69] 出院人数指报告期内所有住院后出院的人数，包括医嘱离院、医嘱转其他医疗机构、非医嘱离院、死亡及其他人数，不含家庭病床撤床人数。

图 23 2014–2018 年年末卫生技术人员人数

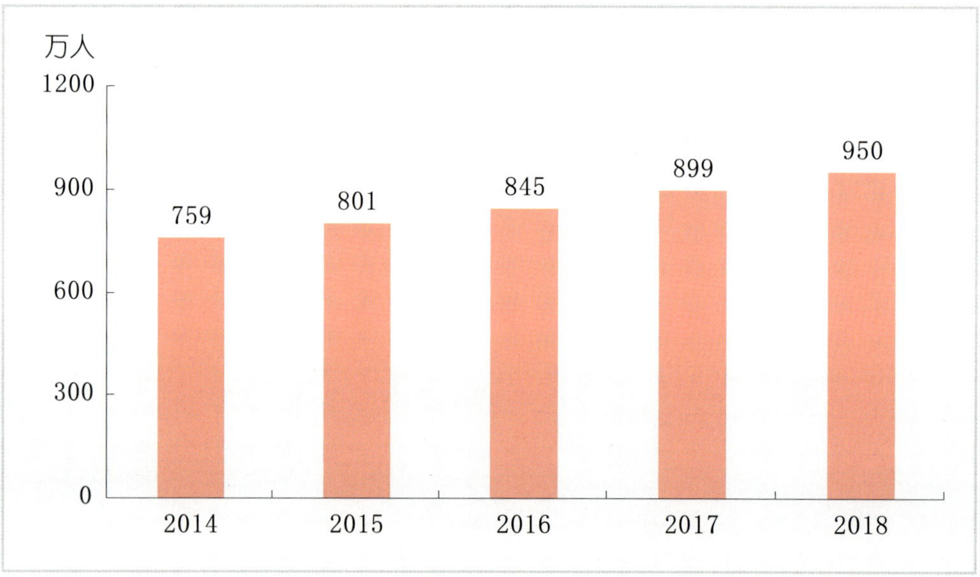

全年我国运动员在24个运动大项中获得118个世界冠军，共创15项世界纪录。全年我国残疾人运动员在20项国际赛事中获得50个世界冠军。

十二、资源、环境和应急管理

全年全国国有建设用地供应总量[70]64.3万公顷，比上年增长6.6%。其中，工矿仓储用地13.2万公顷，增长7.2%；房地产用地[71]14.4万公顷，增长24.6%；基础设施等用地36.8万公顷，增长0.7%。

全年水资源总量27960亿立方米。全年总用水量6110亿立方米，比上年增长1.1%。其中，生活用水增长1.4%，工业用水增长0.6%，农业用水增长1.1%，生态补水增长3.8%。万元国内生产总值用水量[72]73立方米，比上年下降5.1%。万元工业增加值用水量45立方米，下降5.2%。人均用水量439立方米，比上年增长0.6%。

全年完成造林面积707万公顷，其中人工造林面积360万公顷，占全部造林面积的50.9%。森林抚育面积852万公顷。截至年底，国家级自然保护区474个。新增水土流失治理面积5.4万平方公里。

初步核算，全年能源消费总量46.4亿吨标准煤，比上年增长3.3%。煤炭消费量增长1.0%，原油消费量增长6.5%，天然气消费量增长17.7%，电力消费量增长8.5%。煤炭消费量占能源消费

[70] 国有建设用地供应总量是指报告期内市、县人民政府根据年度土地供应计划依法以出让、划拨、租赁等方式将土地使用权提供给单位或个人使用的国有建设用地总量。

[71] 房地产用地是指商服用地和住宅用地的总和。

[72] 万元国内生产总值用水量、万元工业增加值用水量按2015年价格计算。

总量的 59.0%，比上年下降 1.4 个百分点；天然气、水电、核电、风电等清洁能源消费量占能源消费总量的 22.1%，上升 1.3 个百分点。重点耗能工业企业单位烧碱综合能耗下降 0.5%，单位合成氨综合能耗下降 0.7%，吨钢综合能耗下降 3.3%，单位铜冶炼综合能耗下降 4.7%，每千瓦时火力发电标准煤耗下降 0.7%。全国万元国内生产总值二氧化碳排放下降 4.0%。

图 24　2014—2018 年清洁能源消费量占能源消费总量的比重

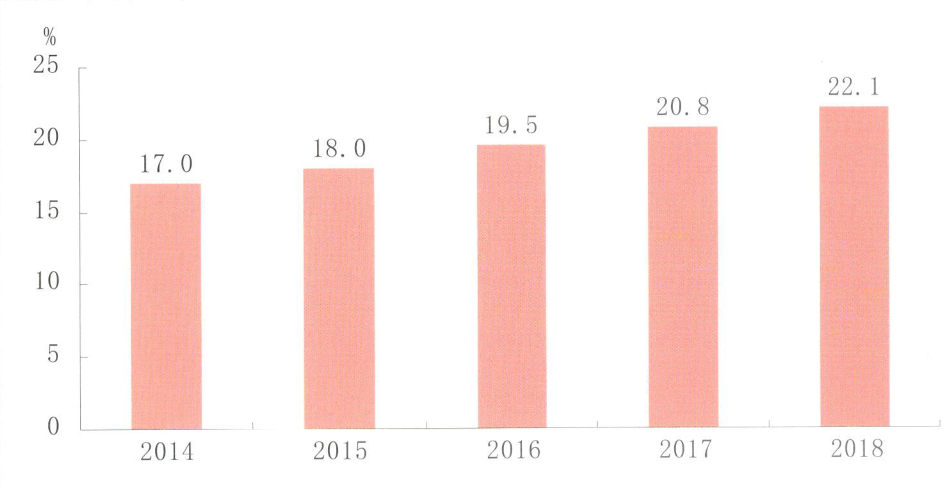

近岸海域 417 个海水水质监测点中，达到国家一、二类海水水质标准的监测点占 74.6%，三类海水占 6.7%，四类、劣四类海水占 18.7%。

在监测的 338 个地级及以上城市中，城市空气质量达标的城市占 35.8%，未达标的城市占 64.2%。细颗粒物（$PM_{2.5}$）未达标城市（基于 2015 年 $PM_{2.5}$ 年平均浓度未达标的 262 个城市）年平均浓度 43 微克／立方米，比上年下降 10.4%。

在开展城市区域声环境监测的 323 个城市中，声环境质量好的城市占 4.0%，较好的占 63.5%，一般的占 30.7%，较差的占 1.2%，差的占 0.6%。

全年平均气温为 10.09℃，比上年下降 0.30℃。共有 10 个台风登陆。

全年农作物受灾面积 2081 万公顷，其中绝收 259 万公顷。全年因洪涝和地质灾害造成直接经济损失 1061 亿元，因旱灾造成直接经济损失 255 亿元，因低温冷冻和雪灾造成直接经济损失 434 亿元，因海洋灾害造成直接经济损失 48 亿元。全年大陆地区共发生 5.0 级以上地震 16 次，成灾 11 次，造成直接经济损失约 30 亿元。全年共发生森林火灾 2478 起，受害森林面积 1.6 万公顷。

全年各类生产安全事故共死亡 34046 人。工矿商贸企业就业人员 10 万人生产安全事故死亡人数 1.547 人，比上年下降 5.6%；煤矿百万吨死亡人数 0.093 人，下降 12.3%。道路交通事故万车死亡人数 1.93 人，下降 6.3%。

资料来源：

本公报中户籍人口城镇化率、民用汽车、道路交通事故数据来自公安部；城镇新增就业、登记失业率、社会保障、技工学校数据来自人力资源和社会保障部；外汇储备、汇率数据来自国家外汇管理局；水产品产量数据来自农业农村部；木材产量、造林面积、森林抚育面积、国家级自然保护区数据来自国家林业和草原局；灌溉面积、水资源、水土流失治理面积数据来自水利部；发电装机容量、新增220千伏及以上变电设备数据来自中国电力企业联合会；港口货物吞吐量、港口集装箱吞吐量、公路运输、水运、新改建公路里程、港口万吨级码头泊位新增通过能力数据来自交通运输部；铁路运输、新建铁路投产里程、增新建铁路复线投产里程、电气化铁路投产里程数据来自中国铁路总公司；民航、新增民用运输机场数据来自中国民用航空局；管道数据来自中国石油天然气集团有限公司、中国石油化工集团有限公司、中国海洋石油集团有限公司；邮政业务数据来自国家邮政局；通信业、软件业务收入、新增光缆线路长度等数据来自工业和信息化部；棚户区改造、农村地区建档立卡贫困户危房改造数据来自住房和城乡建设部；货物进出口数据来自海关总署；服务进出口、外商直接投资、对外直接投资、对外承包工程、对外劳务合作等数据来自商务部；财政数据来自财政部；货币金融、公司信用类债券数据来自中国人民银行；境内交易场所筹资数据来自中国证券监督管理委员会；保险业数据来自中国银行保险监督管理委员会；医疗保险、资助参加基本医疗保险、医疗救助数据来自国家医疗保障局；城乡低保、农村特困人员救助供养、临时救助、社会服务数据来自民政部；优抚对象数据来自退役军人事务部；国家重点研发计划、国家科技重大专项、国家重点实验室、科技成果转化引导基金、技术合同等数据来自科学技术部；国家自然科学基金项目数据来自国家自然科学基金委员会；国家工程研究中心、国家工程实验室、国家企业技术中心等数据来自国家发展和改革委员会；专利数据来自国家知识产权局；宇航发射数据来自国家国防科技工业局；质量检验、国家标准制定修订、制造业产品质量合格率数据来自国家市场监督管理总局；教育数据来自教育部；艺术表演团体、博物馆、公共图书馆、文化馆、图书、旅游数据来自文化和旅游部；电视、广播数据来自国家广播电视总局；电影数据来自国家电影局；报纸、期刊数据来自国家新闻出版署；档案数据来自国家档案局；居民出境数据来自国家移民管理局；医疗卫生数据来自国家卫生健康委员会；体育数据来自国家体育总局；残疾人运动员数据来自中国残疾人联合会；国有建设用地供应、海洋灾害造成直接经济损失数据来自自然资源部；万元国内生产总值二氧化碳排放、环境监测等数据来自生态环境部；平均气温、登陆台风数据来自中国气象局；农作物受灾面积、洪涝和地质灾害造成直接经济损失、旱灾造成直接经济损失、低温冷冻和雪灾造成直接经济损失、森林火灾、受害森林面积、安全生产数据来自应急管理部；地震次数、地震灾害造成直接经济损失数据来自中国地震局；其他数据均来自国家统计局。

STATISTICAL COMMUNIQUÉ OF THE PEOPLE'S REPUBLIC OF CHINA ON THE 2018 NATIONAL ECONOMIC AND SOCIAL DEVELOPMENT[1]

National Bureau of Statistics of China
February 28, 2019

In 2018, in the face of the complicated and severe international environment as well as the daunting and heavy tasks of reform, development and stability, under the strong leadership of the Central Committee of the Communist Party of China with Comrade Xi Jinping as the core and the guidance of Xi Jinping Thought on Socialism with Chinese Characteristics for a New Era, all regions and departments have implemented the spirit of the 19th National Congress of the Communist Party of China and the second and third plenary sessions of the 19th Central Committee of the Communist Party of China, followed the decisions and arrangements made by the CPC Central Committee and the State Council, promoted balanced economic, political, cultural, social and ecological progress, coordinated the implementation of the four-pronged comprehensive strategy, adhered to the general working guideline of making progress while maintaining stability, thoroughly implemented the new development philosophy and committed to the requirement of

1. All figures in this Communiqué are preliminary statistics. Statistics in this Communiqué do not include Hong Kong SAR, Macao SAR and Taiwan Province. Due to the rounding-off reasons, the subentries may not add up to the aggregate totals.

high-quality development. All regions and departments have focused on the supply-side structural reform, deepened the reform and opened wider to the world, unswervingly fought the "three critical battles" of forestalling and defusing major risks, conducting targeted poverty alleviation and preventing and controlling pollution, and coped effectively with the profound changes in the external environment. All regions and departments have coordinated the efforts in stabilizing growth, stimulating reform, adjusting structure, benefiting people's livelihood and fending off risks, and maintained stability in areas like employment, financial sector, foreign trade, foreign investment, domestic investment and market expectation. As a result, the economy was generally stable with growing momentum, the development quality and returns were steadily raised, people's livelihood was further improved, sustainable and healthy economic development and overall social stability were maintained, and new steps were taken towards the goal of completing the building of a moderately prosperous society in all respects.

I. General Outlook

According to preliminary estimation, the gross domestic product (GDP)[2] in 2018 was 90,030.9 billion yuan, up by 6.6 percent over the previous year. Of this total, the value added of the primary industry was 6,473.4 billion yuan, up by 3.5 percent, that of the secondary industry was 36,600.1 billion yuan, up by 5.8 percent and that of the tertiary industry was 46,957.5 billion yuan, up by 7.6 percent. The value added of the primary industry accounted for 7.2 percent of the GDP; that of the secondary industry accounted for 40.7 percent; and that of the tertiary industry accounted for 52.2 percent. The contribution of the final consumption expenditure to GDP accounted for 76.2 percent, that of the gross capital formation 32.4 percent and that of the net exports of goods and services -8.6 percent. The per capita GDP in 2018 was 64,644 yuan, up by 6.1 percent compared with the previous year. The gross national income[3] in 2018 was 89,691.5 billion yuan, up by 6.5 percent over the previous year. The national energy consumption per 10,000 yuan worth of GDP[4] went down by 3.1 percent over 2017, and the overall labor productivity[5] reached 107,327 yuan per person in 2018, up by 6.6 percent over the previous year.

---

2. Gross domestic product (GDP), value added, per capita GDP and gross national income (GNI) as quoted in this Communiqué are calculated at current prices whereas their growth rates are at constant prices. GDP, shares of three industries' value added of GDP, the overall labor productivity and other historical data have been revised based on the results of the third national agricultural census.

3. Gross national income, also known as gross national product, refers to the total primary distribution of the income created by all the resident units of a country (or a region) during a certain period of time. It equals to gross domestic product plus the net primary distribution of income from abroad.

4. The national energy consumption per 10,000 yuan worth of GDP is calculated at constant prices of 2015.

5. The overall labor productivity refers to the ratio between the GDP (at 2015 constant prices) and the total number of persons employed.

Figure 1: Gross Domestic Product and Growth Rates 2014-2018

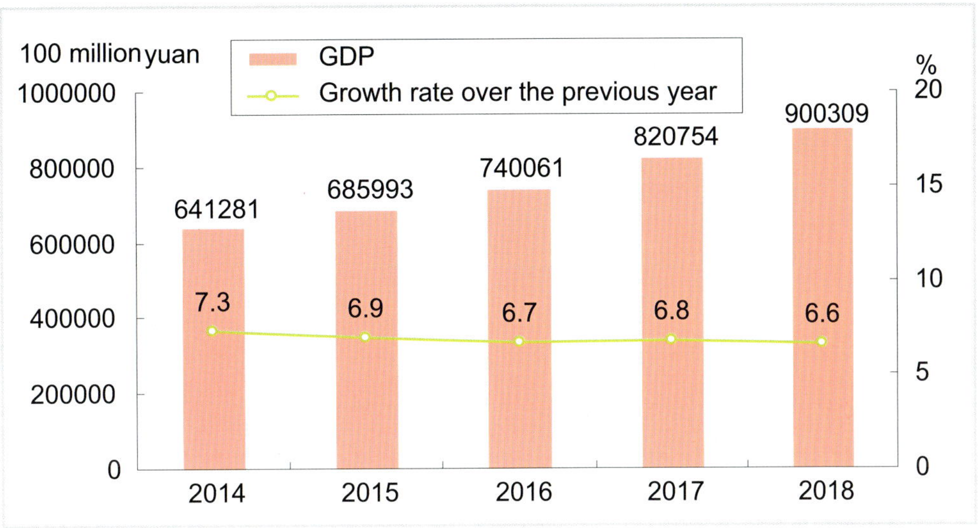

Figure 2: Shares of the Three Industries' Value Added of GDP 2014-2018

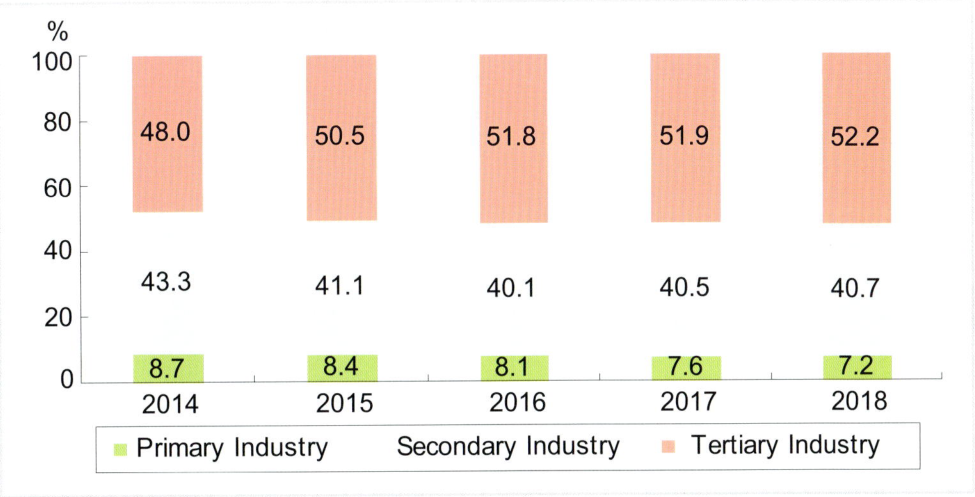

Figure 3: Changes of Energy Consumption per 10,000 Yuan Worth of GDP 2014-2018

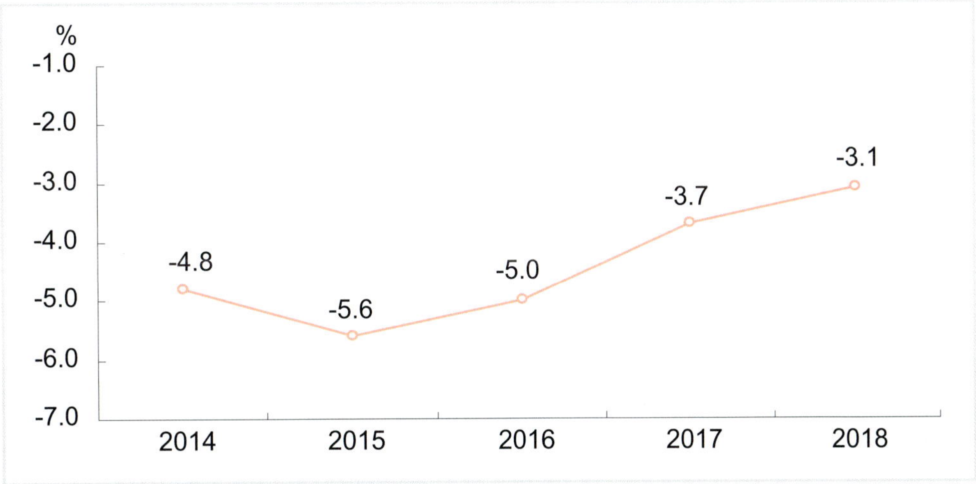

Figure 4: The Overall Labor Productivity 2014-2018

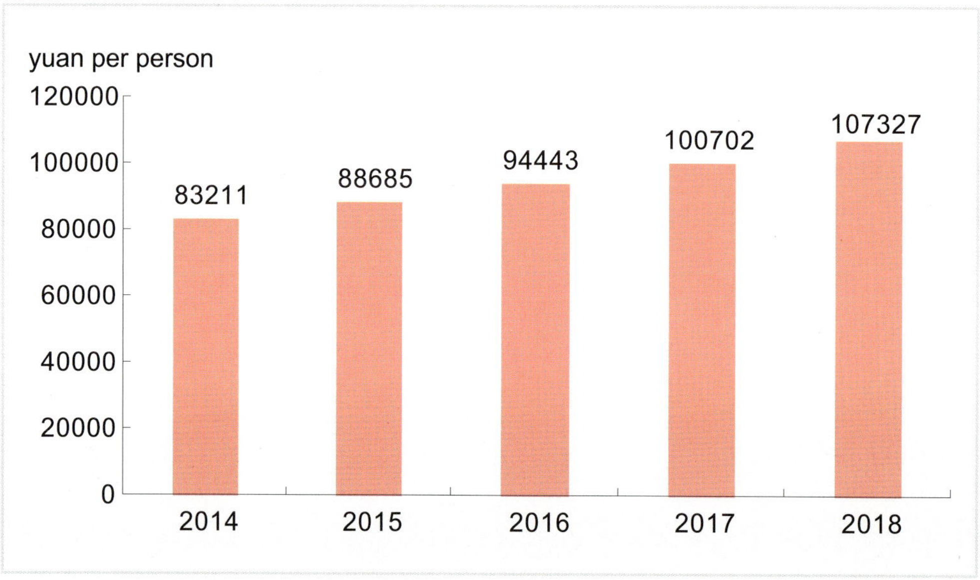

By the end of 2018, the total number of Chinese population at the mainland reached 1,395.38 million, an increase of 5.30 million over that at the end of 2017. Of this total, urban permanent residents numbered 831.37 million, accounting for 59.58 percent of the total population (the urbanization rate of permanent residents), 1.06 percentage points higher than that at the end of 2017. The urbanization rate of population with household registration was 43.37 percent, 1.02 percentage points higher than that at the end of 2017. The year 2018 saw 15.23 million births, a crude birth rate of 10.94 per thousand, and 9.93 million deaths, a crude death rate of 7.13 per thousand. The natural growth rate was 3.81 per thousand. The number of population who live in places other than their household registration areas[6] reached 286 million, of which 241 million were floating population[7].

6. Population who live in places other than their household registration areas refers to those who reside in areas other than their household registration and have been away from there for over 6 months.

7. Floating population refers to the population who live in places other than their household registration excluding those with current residences different from the places of their household registration but still in the same city. Population who live in places other than their household registration but still in the same city refers to those whose current residences are different from the registered towns or streets in the same district or in different districts but still in the same municipality or prefecture-level city.

Table 1: Population and Its Composition by the End of 2018

Item	Population at Year-end (10,000 persons)	Proportion (%)
National Total	**139538**	**100.0**
Of which: Urban	83137	59.58
Rural	56401	40.42
Of which: Male	71351	51.1
Female	68187	48.9
Of which: Aged 0-15 (under the age of 16)[8]	24860	17.8
Aged 16-59 (under the age of 60)	89729	64.3
Aged 60 and above	24949	17.9
Of which: Aged 65 and above	16658	11.9

At the end of 2018, the number of employed people in China was 775.86 million, and that in urban areas was 434.19 million. The newly increased employed people in urban areas numbered 13.61 million, 0.10 million more than the previous year. The surveyed urban unemployment rate was 4.9 percent at the year end, 0.1 percentage point lower than the end of 2017. The registered urban unemployment rate was 3.8 percent, 0.1 percentage point lower. The total number of migrant workers[9] in 2018 was 288.36 million, up by 0.6 percent over that of 2017. Specifically, the number of migrant workers who left their hometowns and worked in other places was 172.66 million, up by 0.5 percent, and those who worked in their own localities reached 115.70 million, up by 0.9 percent.

Figure 5: Newly Increased Employed People in Urban Areas 2014-2018

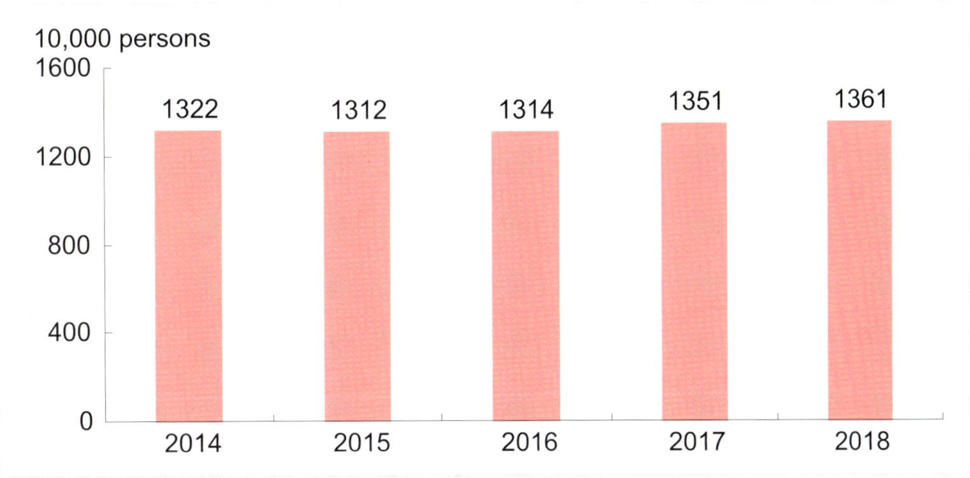

8. By the end of 2018, the population aged 0 to 14 (under the age of 15) was 235.23 million and that aged 15 to 59 (under the age of 60) was 910.66 million.

9. The number of migrant workers includes those who are employed outside their villages and towns for more than six months in the year and those who do non-agricultural work in their villages and towns for more than six months in the year.

The consumer prices in 2018 went up by 2.1 percent over the previous year. The producer prices went up by 3.5 percent and the purchasing prices for manufactured goods up by 4.1 percent. The prices for investment in fixed assets increased by 5.4 percent. The producer prices for farm products[10] decreased by 0.9 percent. In December, out of the 70 large-and-medium-sized cities, 69 cities experienced a year-on-year rise in sales prices of new commercial residential buildings and one city experienced a decline.

Figure 6: Monthly Changes of Consumer Prices in 2018

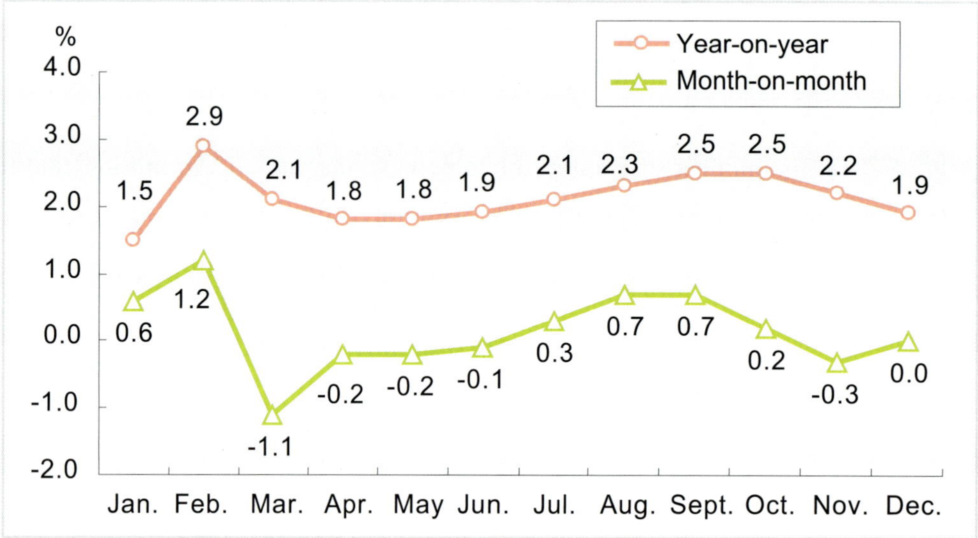

Table 2: Changes of Consumer Prices in 2018

Unit: %

Item	National Average	Urban	Rural
General level of consumer prices	**2.1**	**2.1**	**2.1**
Of which: Food, tobacco and liquor	1.9	2.1	1.1
Clothing	1.2	1.1	1.5
Residence[11]	2.4	2.1	3.3
Household facilities, articles and services	1.6	1.6	1.6
Transportation and telecommunication	1.7	1.6	1.8
Education, culture and recreation	2.2	2.3	2.2
Health care and medical services	4.3	4.6	3.7
Miscellaneous goods and services	1.2	1.2	1.2

10. The producer prices for farm products refer to the prices of farm products sold directly by producers.
11. The prices for residence include prices for rent, maintenance and management, water, electricity and fuel etc.

At the end of 2018, China's foreign exchange reserves reached 3,072.7 billion US dollars, 67.2 billion US dollars less compared with that at the end of 2017. The average exchange rate of the year was 6.6174 RMB to 1 USD dollar, appreciated by 2.0 percent over that of 2017.

Figure 7: Year-end China's Foreign Exchange Reserves 2014-2018

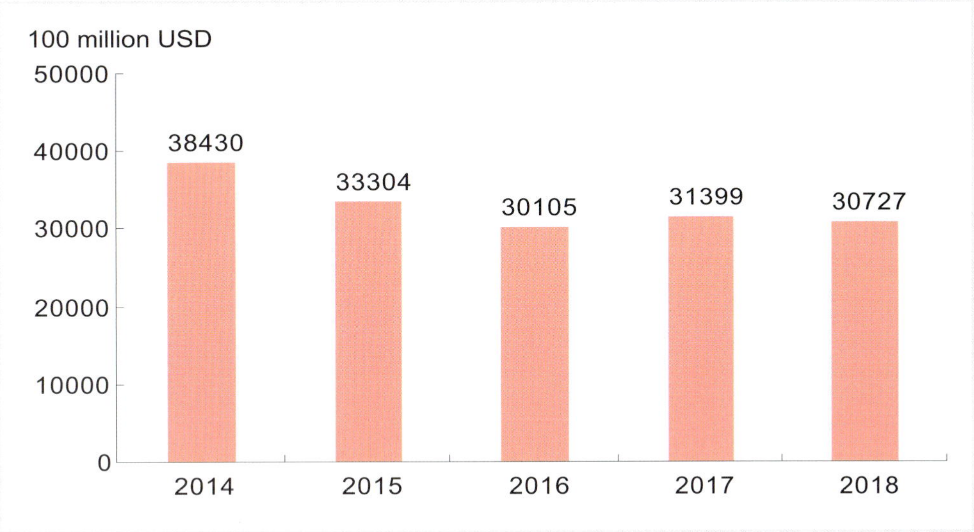

The supply-side structural reform was further pushed forward. The national industrial capacity utilization rate[12] in 2018 reached 76.5 percent. Specifically, the capacity utilization rate for mining and washing of coal was 70.6 percent, 2.4 percentage points higher than the previous year and that for smelting and pressing of ferrous metals was 78.0 percent, 2.2 percentage points higher. The floor space of commercial buildings for sale at the end of 2018 was 524.14 million square meters, 65.10 million square meters less than that at the end of 2017. Of this total, the floor space of the commercial residential buildings for sale was 250.91 million square meters, 50.72 million square meters less. The asset-liability ratio of the industrial enterprises above the designated size at the end of 2018 was 56.5 percent, 0.5 percentage point[13] less than that at the end of 2017. The cost for per-hundred-yuan turnover of principal activities of the industrial enterprises above the designated size was 83.88 yuan in 2018, 0.20 yuan less compared with the previous year. In

12. Capacity utilization rate refers to the ratio of the actual production to the production capacity (in terms of value). Actual production refers to the total industrial output value during the enterprise's reporting period. Production capacity refers to the production which can be realized and sustained for a long term under the condition of the supply of labor force, materials, fuel and transportation guaranteed and the production equipment in proper operation.

13. The growth rates and rate changes of financial indicators of industrial enterprises above the designated size of 2018 are calculated on a comparable basis due to adjustments of data coverage in the statistical programmes, statistical law enforcement, removal of duplicated data, corporate reforms and divestiture etc.

2018, the fixed assets investment (excluding by rural households) in ecological protection and treatment of environmental pollution and in agriculture went up by 43.0 percent and 15.4 percent respectively compared with 2017.

The new driving forces continued to grow. Among the industries above the designated size, the value added of the strategic emerging industries[14] grew by 8.9 percent over the previous year and the value added of the high technology manufacturing industry[15] was up by 11.7 percent over the previous year, accounting for 13.9 percent of that of all industrial enterprises above the designated size. The value added for the manufacture of equipment[16] was up by 8.1 percent, accounting for 32.9 percent of that of all industrial enterprises above the designated size. Among the service enterprises above the designated size[17], the business revenue of the strategic emerging service industries[18] went up by 14.6 percent compared with the previous year. In 2018, the investment in high technology industries[19] increased by 14.9 percent over the previous year; the investment in industrial technological transformation[20] increased by 12.8 percent. In 2018, the production of new energy vehicles reached 1.15 million, up by 66.2 percent compared with the previous year and that of smart TV sets 113.76 million, up by 17.7 percent. In 2018, the online retail sales[21] reached 9,006.5 billion yuan, an increase of 23.9 percent.

---

14. Industrial strategic emerging industries refer to the related industrial sectors of energy-saving and environmental protection, information technology of new generation, biotech, manufacture of high-end equipment, new energy, new materials, and new energy vehicles.

15. High technology manufacturing industry includes manufacture of medicine, manufacture of aerospace vehicle and equipment, manufacture of electronic and communication equipment, manufacture of computers and office equipment, manufacture of medical equipment, manufacture of measuring instrument and equipment and manufacture of optical and photographic equipment.

16. Manufacture of equipment includes manufacture of metal products, general purpose equipment, special purpose equipment, automobiles, railway, ship, aerospace and other transport equipment, electrical machinery and apparatus, computers, communication and other electric equipment and measuring instrument and machinery.

17. Service enterprises above the designated size, refer to legal entities of transport, storage and post, information transmission, software and information technology services, real estate (excluding real estate development and operation), leasing and business services, scientific research and technical services, water conservancy, environment and public facilities management, education, health and social work with annual business revenue of 10 million yuan and above or with 50 employees and above at the end of the year; legal entities of services to households, repair and other services and culture, sports and entertainment with annual business revenue of 5 million and above or with 50 employees and above at the end of the year.

18. Strategic emerging service industries refer to the related service sectors of energy-saving and environmental protection, information technology of new generation, biotech, manufacture of high-end equipment, new energy, new materials, and new energy vehicles.

19. Investment in high technology industries refers to investment in six high technology manufacturing industries, including the manufacture of medicine and manufacture of aerospace vehicle and equipment, and nine high technology service industries, including information service and e-commerce service.

20. Investment in industrial technological transformation refers to the investment in the improvement of the existing equipments, technologies and production services through new technologies, crafts, equipments and materials so as to achieve intensive development.

21. Online retail sales refer to the retail sales of goods and services realized through internet trading platforms (online platforms mainly in trading physical commodities, including self-built websites and third-party platforms). The growth rate of online retail sales in 2018 was calculated on a comparable basis.

Significant achievement has been made in poverty alleviation. By the rural poverty line of annual per capita income of 2,300 yuan (at 2010 constant prices), the number of rural population living in poverty at the end of 2018 was 16.60 million, 13.86 million[22] less compared with that at the end of 2017, and the incidence of poverty[23] was 1.7 percent, 1.4 percentage points lower than that of the previous year. In 2018, the per capita disposable income of rural residents in impoverished areas[24] was 10,371 yuan, an increase of 10.6 percent over 2017, or a real increase of 8.3 percent after price adjustment.

Figure 8: Year-end Rural Population in Poverty and Incidence of Poverty 2014-2018

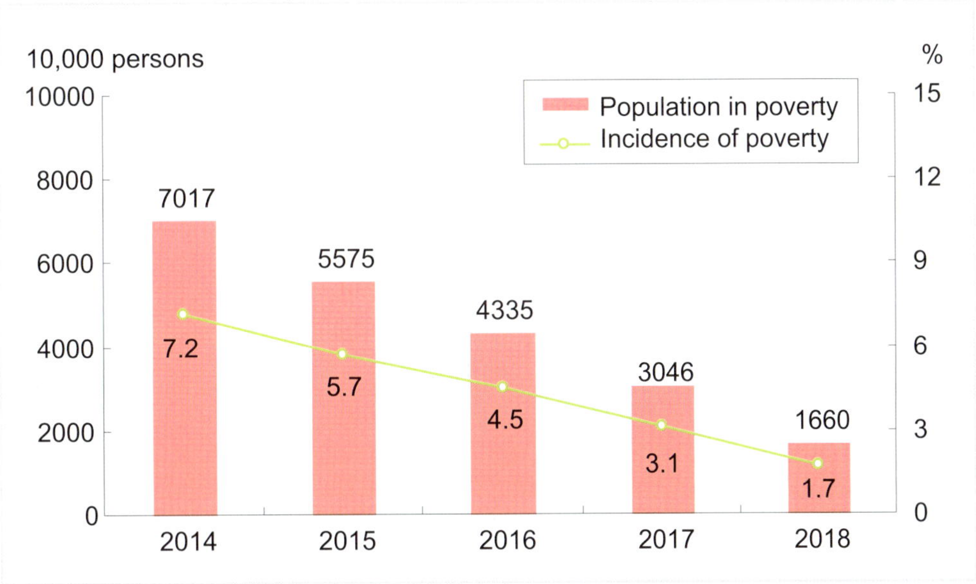

II. Agriculture[25]

In 2018, the sown area of grain was 117.04 million hectares, a drop of 0.95 million hectares compared with that in 2017. Of this total, the sown area of wheat was 24.27 million hectares, a decrease of 0.24 million

22. The number of people lifted out of poverty equals the population in poverty in the current year minus that in the previous year. It is also equivalent to the population out of poverty minus the population returning to poverty in the current year.
23. The incidence of poverty refers to the proportion of population in poverty to targeted population under survey.
24. Impoverished areas cover contiguous poverty-stricken areas and key counties under national poverty alleviation and development program beyond those areas. There were 832 counties altogether. Since 2017, Aksu prefecture in Xinjiang has also been covered in poverty monitoring.
25. Historical data of agriculture, animal husbandry and fishery have been revised based on the results of the third national agricultural census.

hectares; the sown area of rice was 30.19 million hectares, a decrease of 0.56 million hectares; the sown area of corn was 42.13 million hectares, a decrease of 0.27 million hectares. The sown area of cotton was 3.35 million hectares, an increase of 0.16 million hectares. The sown area of oil-bearing crops was 12.89 million hectares, a decrease of 0.33 million hectares; the sown area of sugar crops was 1.63 million hectares, an increase of 90 thousand hectares.

The total output of grain in 2018 was 657.89 million tons, a decrease of 3.71 million tons or down by 0.6 percent over the previous year. Of this total, the output of summer crops was 138.78 million tons, down by 2.1 percent, and that of the early rice was 28.59 million tons, down by 4.3 percent over the previous year. The output of autumn grain was 490.52 million tons, up by 0.1 percent. The output of cereal was 610.19 million tons, down by 0.8 percent over 2017, among which the output of rice was 212.13 million tons, down by 0.3 percent; that of wheat was 131.43 million tons, down by 2.2 percent; and that of corn was 257.33 million tons, down by 0.7 percent.

Figure 9: Output of Grain 2014-2018

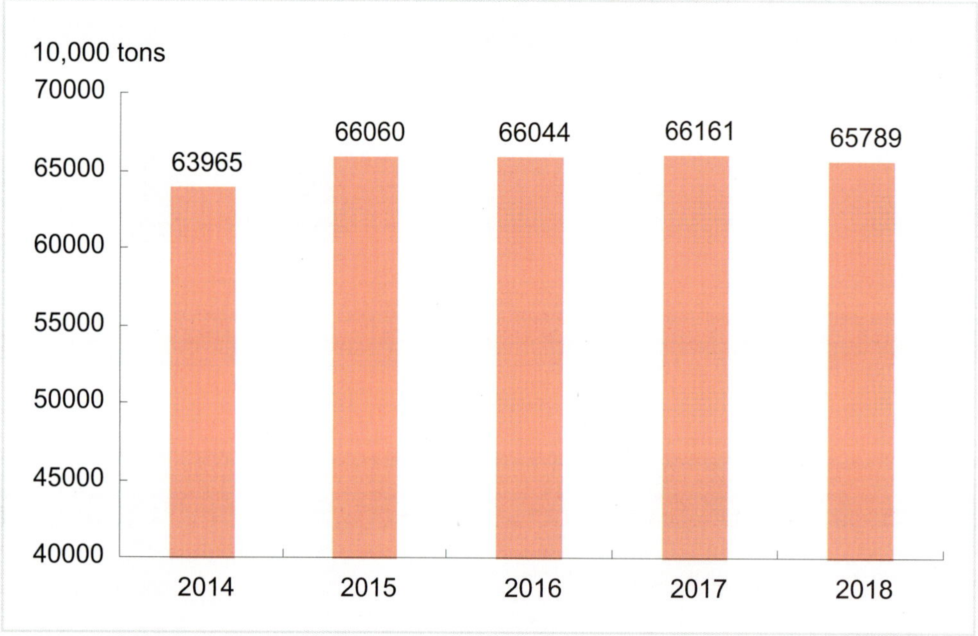

In 2018, the output of cotton was 6.10 million tons, an increase of 7.8 percent over the previous year, that of oil-bearing crops was 34.39 million tons, down by 1.0 percent, that of sugar crops was 119.76 million tons, up by 5.3 percent, and that of tea was 2.61 million tons, up by 5.9 percent.

The total output of pork, beef, mutton and poultry in 2018 reached 85.17 million tons, down by 0.3 percent over the previous year. Of this total, the output of pork was 54.04 million tons, down by 0.9 percent; that of beef was 6.44 million tons, up by 1.5 percent; that of mutton was 4.75 million tons, up by 0.8 percent; and that of poultry was 19.94 million tons, up by 0.6 percent. The total output of eggs was 31.28 million tons, up by 1.0 percent. The production of milk was 30.75 million tons, up by 1.2 percent. At the end of the year, 428.17 million pigs were registered in the total stocks, down by 3.0 percent, and 693.82 million pigs were slaughtered, down by 1.2 percent.

The total output of aquatic products in 2018 was 64.69 million tons, up by 0.4 percent over the previous year. Of this total, the output of cultured aquatic products was 50.18 million tons, up by 2.3 percent; and that of fished aquatic products was 14.51 million tons, down by 5.7 percent over the previous year.

The total production of timber for 2018 reached 84.32 million cubic meters, up by 0.4 percent over the previous year.

In 2018, over 0.72 million hectares of farmland were newly equipped with effective irrigation systems and another 1.44 million hectares of farmland was newly equipped with water-saving irrigation systems.

III. Industry and Construction

In 2018, the total value added of the industrial sector was 30,516.0 billion yuan, up by 6.1 percent over the previous year. The value added of industrial enterprises above the designated size increased by 6.2 percent. Of the industrial enterprises above the designated size, in terms of ownership, the value added of the state-holding enterprises grew by 6.2 percent, that of the share-holding enterprises up by 6.6 percent, that of the enterprises by foreign investors and investors from Hong Kong, Macao and Taiwan up by 4.8 percent and that of private enterprises up by 6.2 percent. In terms of sectors, the value added of the mining industry was up by 2.3 percent, that of manufacturing up by 6.5 percent and that of production and supply of electricity, heat power, gas and water up by 9.9 percent.

Figure 10: Value Added and Growth Rates of Industrial Enterprises 2014-2018

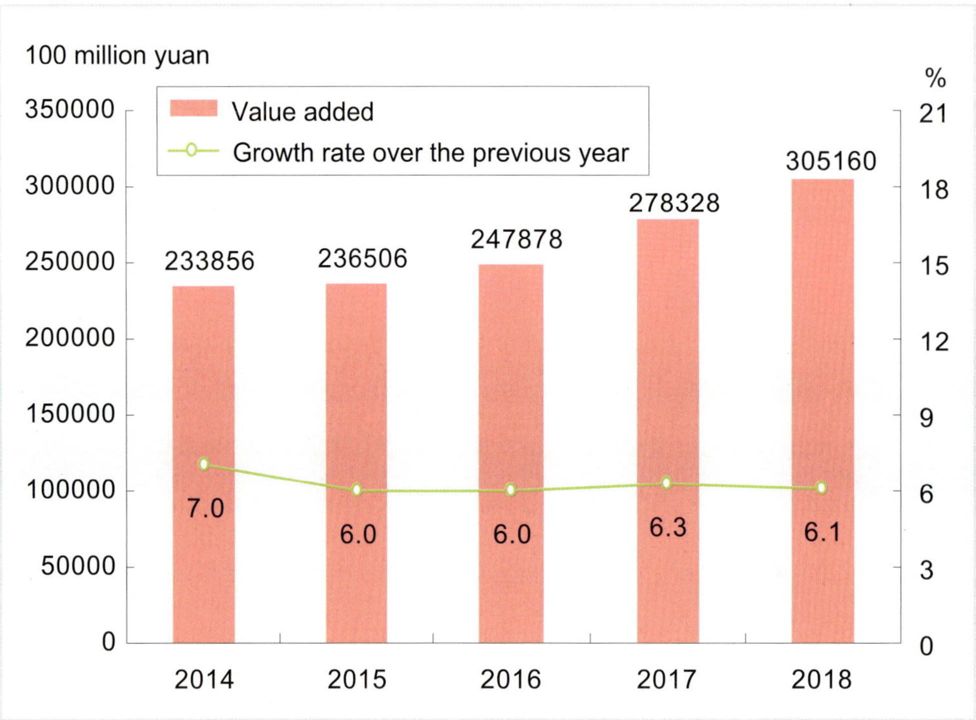

In 2018, of the industrial enterprises above the designated size, the value added for processing of food from agricultural and sideline products was up by 5.9 percent over the previous year; for textile industry up by 1.0 percent; for manufacture of raw chemical materials and chemical products up by 3.6 percent; for manufacture of non-metallic mineral products up by 4.6 percent; for smelting and pressing of ferrous metals up by 7.0 percent; for manufacture of general purpose machinery up by 7.2 percent; for manufacture of special purpose machinery up by 10.9 percent; for manufacture of automobiles up by 4.9 percent; for manufacture of electrical machinery and apparatus up by 7.3 percent; for manufacture of computers, communication equipment and other electronic equipment up by 13.1 percent; for production and supply of electricity and heat power up by 9.6 percent.

Table 3: Output of Major Industrial Products and Growth Rates in 2018[26]

Product	Unit	Output	Increase over 2017 (%)
Yarn	10000 tons	2958.9	-7.3
Cloth	100 million meters	657.3	-4.9
Chemical fiber	10000 tons	5011.1	2.7
Refined sugar (final product)	10000 tons	1524.1	3.5
Cigarettes	100 million	23358.7	-0.4
Color TV sets	10000	18834.8	18.2
Of which: LCD TV sets	10000	18825.2	19.5
Household refrigerators	10000	7993.2	-3.9
Air conditioners	10000	20486.0	14.7
Primary energy output	100 million tons of standard coal equivalent	37.7	5.0
Coal	100 million tons	36.8	4.5
Crude petroleum oil	10000 tons	18910.6	-1.3
Natural gas	100 million cubic meters	1602.7	8.3
Electricity	100 million kilowatt-hours	71117.7	7.7
Of which: Thermal power[27]	100 million kilowatt-hours	50738.6	6.7
Hydropower	100 million kilowatt-hours	12342.3	3.0
Nuclear-power	100 million kilowatt-hours	2943.6	18.7
Crude steel	10000 tons	92800.9	6.6
Rolled steel[28]	10000 tons	110551.7	5.6
Ten kinds of nonferrous metals	10000 tons	5702.7	3.7
Of which: Refined copper (copper)	10000 tons	902.9	0.7
Aluminum electrolyze	10000 tons	3580.2	7.5
Cement	100 million tons	22.1	-5.3
Sulfuric acid (100%)	10000 tons	9129.8	-0.9
Caustic soda (100%)	10000 tons	3420.2	2.7
Ethylene	10000 tons	1841.0	1.1
Chemical fertilizers (100 percent equivalent)	10000 tons	5424.4	-7.9
Power generation equipment	10000 kilowatts	10600.5	-10.3
Motor vehicles	10000	2781.9	-4.1
Of which: Basic passenger cars (cars)	10000	1160.1	-2.9
Sport utility vehicles (SUVs)	10000	927.4	-7.7
Large and medium tractors	10000	24.3	-29.3
Integrated circuits	100 million pieces	1739.5	11.2
Program-controlled switchboards	10000 lines	1006.6	7.3
Mobile telephones	10000	179846.4	-4.8
Micro computer equipment	10000	30700.2	0.1
Industrial Robots	10000 sets	14.8	6.4

26. Output data of some products were reviewed and revised in 2017; therefore the growth rates of output in 2018 were calculated on a comparable basis by applying the revised data.
27. Thermal power refers to electricity generated by coal, oil, gas, residual heat, pressure and gas, waste incineration and biomass.
28. The data include 218.00 million tons of steel which has been reprocessed among enterprises.

By the end of 2018, the installed power generation capacity was 1,899.67 million kilowatts, up by 6.5 percent[29] over that at the end of 2017, among which[30] the installed thermal power generation capacity was 1,143.67 million kilowatts, up by 3.0 percent; the installed hydropower generation capacity was 352.26 million kilowatts, up by 2.5 percent; the installed nuclear power generation capacity was 44.66 million kilowatts, up by 24.7 percent. The installed grid-connected wind power generation capacity was 184.26 million kilowatts, up by 12.4 percent and the installed grid-connected solar power generation capacity was 174.63 million kilowatts, up by 33.9 percent.

In 2018, the profits made by industrial enterprises above the designated size were 6,635.1 billion yuan, up by 10.3 percent[31] over the previous year. By ownership, the profits of state-holding enterprises were 1,858.3 billion yuan, up by 12.6 percent over the previous year; those of share-holding enterprises were 4,697.5 billion yuan, up by 14.4 percent; those of enterprises funded by foreign investors or investors from Hong Kong, Macao and Taiwan were 1,677.6 billion yuan, up by 1.9 percent; and those of private enterprises was 1,713.7 billion yuan, up by 11.9 percent. In terms of different sectors, the profits of mining were 524.6 billion yuan, up by 40.1 percent over the previous year; those of manufacturing were 5,696.4 billion yuan, up by 8.7 percent; and those of the production and supply of electricity, heat power, gas and water were 414.1 billion yuan, up by 4.3 percent. In 2018, the profit rate of the principal activities of the industrial enterprises above the designated size was 6.49 percent, 0.11 percentage point higher than that of 2017.

In 2018, the value added of construction enterprises in China was 6,180.8 billion yuan, up by 4.5 percent over the previous year. The profits made by construction enterprises qualified for general contracts and specialized contracts reached 810.4 billion yuan, up by 8.2 percent, of which the profits made by state-holding enterprises were 247.0 billion yuan, up by 8.5 percent.

29. The growth rate was calculated on a comparable basis as China Electricity Council has changed its statistical coverage in 2018.
30. Some installed power generation capacity was not listed (e.g. geothermal).
31. See note 13.

Figure 11: Value Added and Growth Rates of Construction Industry 2014-2018

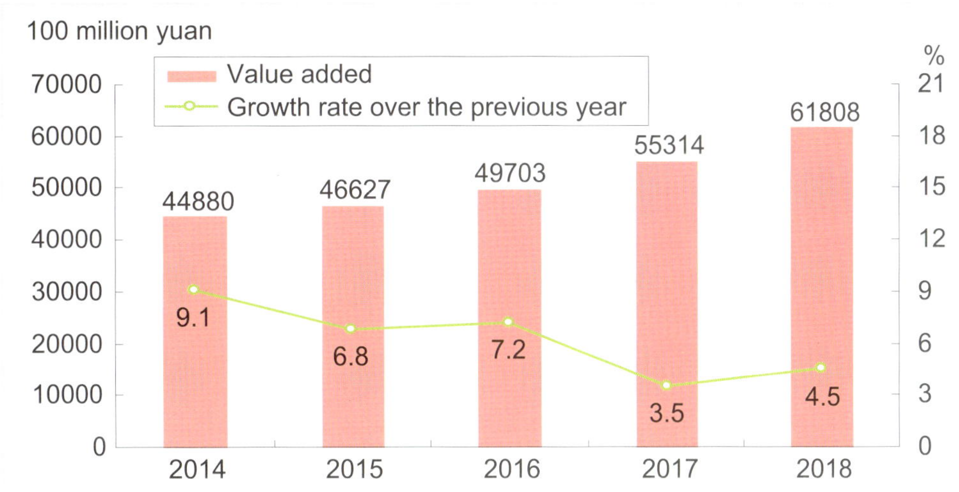

IV. Service Sector

In 2018, the value added of wholesale and retail trades was 8,420.1 billion yuan, up by 6.2 percent over the previous year; that of transport, storage and post was 4,055.0 billion yuan, up by 8.1 percent; that of hotels and catering services was 1,602.3 billion yuan, up by 6.5 percent; that of financial intermediation was 6,910.0 billion yuan, up by 4.4 percent; that of real estate was 5,984.6 billion yuan, up by 3.8 percent; that of information transmission, software and information technology services was 3,243.1 billion yuan, up by 30.7 percent; and that of leasing and business services was 2,442.7 billion yuan, up by 8.9 percent. In 2018, the business revenue of service enterprises above the designated size grew by 11.4 percent over the previous year, and the operating profits grew by 6.5 percent.

Figure 12: Value Added and Growth Rates of Service Sector 2014-2018

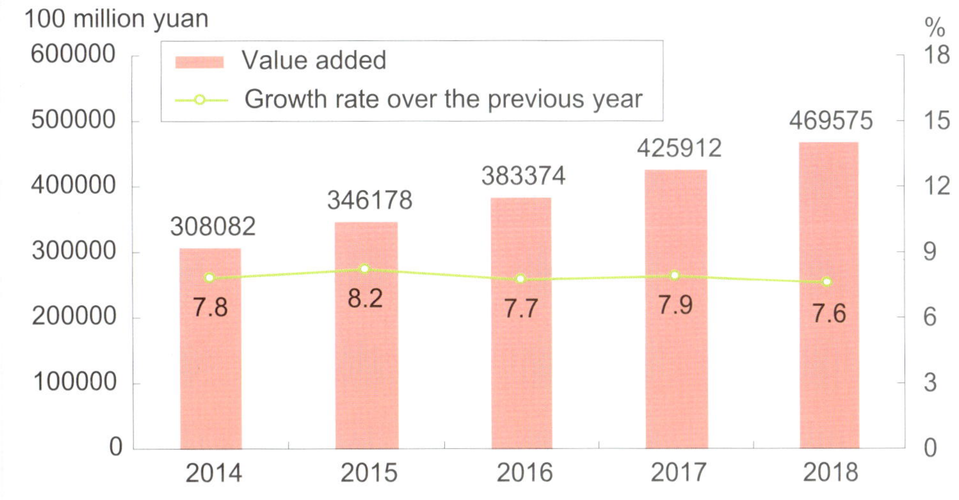

The total freight traffic in 2018 reached 51.5 billion tons, up by 7.1 percent over 2017. The freight flows were 20,545.2 billion ton-kilometers, up by 4.1 percent. The volume of freight handled by ports above the designated size throughout the year totaled 13.3 billion tons, up by 2.7 percent[32] over the previous year, of which the freight for foreign trade was 4.2 billion tons, up by 2.0 percent. Container shipping of ports above the designated size reached 249.55 million standard containers, up by 5.2 percent.

Table 4: Freight Traffic by All Means of Transportation and Growth Rates in 2018

Item	Unit	Volume	Increase over 2017(%)
Total freight traffic	**100 million tons**	**514.6**	**7.1**
Railways	100 million tons	40.3	9.2
Highways	100 million tons	395.9	7.4
Waterways	100 million tons	69.9	4.7
Civil aviation	10 000 tons	738.5	4.6
Pipelines	100 million tons	8.5	5.4
Freight flows	**100 million ton-kilometers**	**205451.6**	**4.1**
Railways	100 million ton-kilometers	28821.0	6.9
Highways	100 million ton-kilometers	71202.5	6.6
Waterways	100 million ton-kilometers	99303.6	0.7
Civil aviation	100 million ton-kilometers	262.4	7.7
Pipelines	100 million ton-kilometers	5862.0	22.5

In 2018, the total passenger traffic[33] reached 17.9 billion person-times, down by 3.1 percent over 2017, and the passenger flows were 3,421.3 billion person-kilometers, up by 4.3 percent.

Table 5: Passenger Traffic by All Means of Transportation and Growth Rates in 2018

Item	Unit	Volume	Increase over 2017(%)
Total passenger traffic	**100 million person-times**	**179.2**	**-3.1**
Railways	100 million person-times	33.7	9.4
Highways	100 million person-times	136.5	-6.3
Waterways	100 million person-times	2.8	-0.5
Civil aviation	100 million person-times	6.1	10.9
Passenger flows	**100 million person-kilometers**	**34213.5**	**4.3**
Railways	100 million person-kilometers	14146.6	5.1
Highways	100 million person-kilometers	9275.5	-5.0
Waterways	100 million person-kilometers	79.8	2.7
Civil aviation	100 million person-kilometers	10711.6	12.6

32. In 2018, the statistical coverage of the volume of freight handled by some ports above the designated size was expanded to all enterprise at the ports; therefore the growth rates of relevant indicators were calculated on a comparable basis.

33. The total passenger traffic includes passenger traffic by railways, highways, waterways and civil aviation for commercial purpose, of which traffic by highways accounted for more than 70 percent. Over recent years, the revolution of people's travel methods has brought about the fast growth of road trips, online car hailing and carpooling, which has caused a decline of the passenger traffic by highways, as well as the total passenger traffic.

The total number of motor vehicles for civilian use reached 240.28 million (including 9.06 million tri-wheel motor vehicles and low-speed trucks) by the end of 2018, up by 10.5 percent over that at the end of 2017, of which the privately-owned vehicles numbered 207.30 million, up by 10.9 percent. The total number of cars for civilian use was 134.51 million, up by 10.4 percent, of which the privately-owned cars numbered 125.89 million, up by 10.3 percent.

The turnover of post services[34] totaled 1,234.5 billion yuan, up by 26.4 percent over the previous year. The number of mail delivery was 2.68 billion; that of parcel delivery was 20 million; and that of express delivery was 50.71 billion with a revenue reaching 603.8 billion yuan. The turnover of telecommunication services[35] totaled 6,555.6 billion yuan, up by 137.9 percent over the previous year. The newly increased capacity of mobile phone switchboard[36] was 172.67 million lines with the total capacity reaching 2,594.53 million lines. By the end of 2018, there were 1,748.35 million phone subscribers in China, of whom 1,566.10 million were mobile phone users. Mobile phone coverage rose to 112.2 sets per 100 persons. The number of fixed broadband internet users[37] reached 407.38 million, increased by 58.84 million over the previous year. Of this total, fixed fiber-optic broadband internet users[38] amounted to 368.33 million, an increase of 74.40 million; and the mobile broadband users[39] numbered 1,305.65 million, an increase of 174.13 million. The mobile internet traffic in 2018 was 71.1 billion gigabytes, up by 189.1 percent over the previous year. Software revenue from software and information technology services industry[40] in 2018 was 6,306.1 billion yuan, up by 14.2 percent over 2017 on a comparable basis.

34. The turnover of post services is calculated at constant prices of 2010.

35. The turnover of telecommunication services is calculated at constant prices of 2015.

36. The capacity of mobile phone switchboard refers to the number of maximum concurrent users calculated by mobile phone switchboard according to selected calling models and switchboard processing capacity.

37. Fixed broadband internet users refer to those who subscribed to the telecommunication enterprises and access the Internet through xDSL, FTTx+LAN, FTTH/0 and other broadband access ways as well as general dedicated lines at the end of the reporting period.

38. Fixed fiber-optic broadband internet users refer to those who subscribed to the telecommunication enterprises and access the Internet through FTTH or FTT0 at the end of the reporting period.

39. Mobile broadband users refer to those who have records in the billing system and use 3G or 4G network resources at the end of the reporting period.

40. Software and information technology services industry includes software development, integrated circuit design, information system integration and internet of things technology services, operation maintenance services, information processing and storage support services, IT consulting services, digital content services and other IT services industry.

Figure 13: Express Delivery and Growth Rates 2014-2018

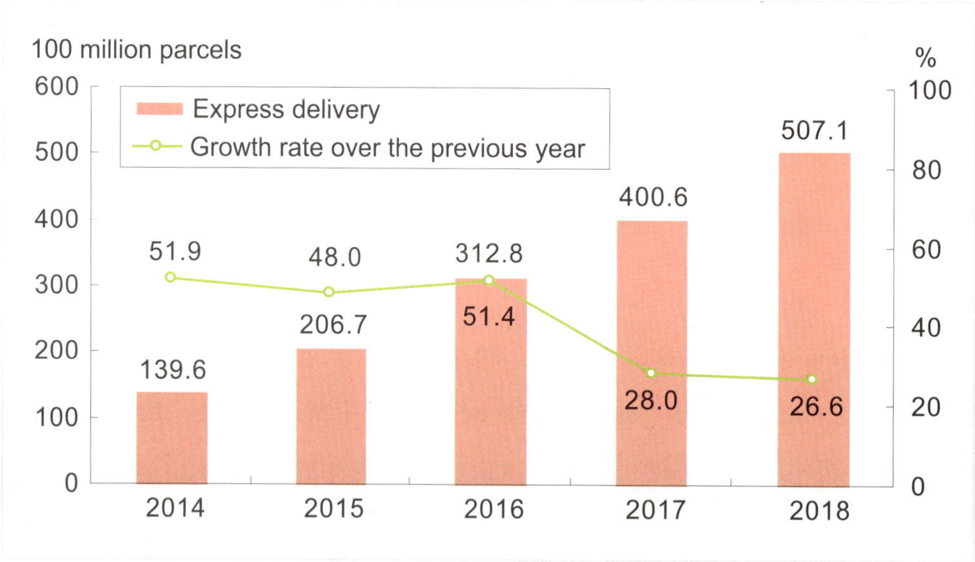

Figure 14: Year-end Number of Fixed Broandband Internet Users and Mobile Broadband Users 2014-2018

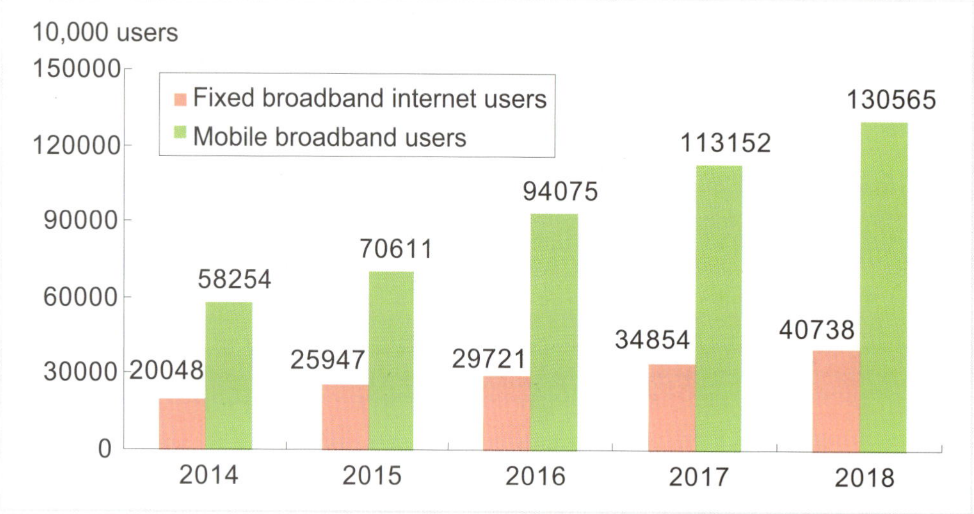

V. Domestic Trade[41]

In 2018, the total retail sales of consumer goods reached 38,098.7 billion yuan, a growth of 9.0 percent over the previous year. An analysis on different areas showed that the retail sales of consumer goods in urban areas stood at 32,563.7 billion yuan, up by 8.8 percent, and that in rural areas reached 5,535.0 billion yuan, up by 10.1 percent. Grouped by consumption patterns, the retail sales of commodities was 33,827.1 billion

41. The total retail sales of consumer goods and the subentries in 2017 have been revised as base data according to the results of the third national agricultural census and related regulations. The growth rates of 2018 were calculated on a comparable basis.

yuan, up by 8.9 percent, and that of catering industry was 4,271.6 billion yuan, up by 9.5 percent.

Of the total retail sales of commodities by enterprises above the designated size, the year-on-year growth of sales for grain, oil and food went up by 10.2 percent; beverage up by 9.0 percent; tobacco and liquor up by 7.4 percent; clothes, shoes, hats and textiles up by 8.0 percent; cosmetics up by 9.6 percent; gold, silver and jewelry up by 7.4 percent; daily necessities up by 13.7 percent; household appliances and audio-video equipments up by 8.9 percent; traditional Chinese and western medicines up by 9.4 percent; cultural and office appliances up by 3.0 percent; furniture up by 10.1 percent; telecommunication equipments up by 7.1 percent; building and decoration materials up by 8.1 percent; petroleum and petroleum products up by 13.3 percent; and motor vehicles down by 2.4 percent.

In 2018, the online retail sales of physical goods were 7,019.8 billion yuan, up by 25.4 percent over the previous year, accounting for 18.4 percent of the total retail sales of consumer goods, or 3.4 percentage points higher than that of 2017.

VI. Investment in Fixed Assets[42]

The total investment in fixed assets of the country in 2018 was 64,567.5 billion yuan, up by 5.9 percent over the previous year. Of the total investment, the investment in fixed assets (excluding by rural households) was 63,563.6 billion yuan, up by 5.9 percent. By regions[43], the investment in eastern areas was up by 5.7 percent over the previous year, central areas up by 10.0 percent, western areas up by 4.7 percent, and northeastern areas up by 1.0 percent.

In the investment in fixed assets (excluding by rural households), the investment in the primary industry was 2,241.3 billion yuan, up by 12.9 percent; that in the secondary industry was 23,789.9 billion yuan, up by 6.2 percent; and that in the tertiary industry was 37,532.4 billion yuan, up by 5.5 percent. The private investment in fixed assets[44] was 39,405.1 billion yuan, up by 8.7 percent, accounting for 62.0 percent of the

42. The base figure of the investment in fixed assets in 2017 was revised according to statistical law enforcement and inspection and the results from the entities inventory checking of the fourth economic census. The growth rates in 2018 were calculated on a comparable basis.

43. The eastern areas include 10 provinces and municipalities: Beijing, Tianjin, Hebei, Shanghai, Jiangsu, Zhejiang, Fujian, Shandong, Guangdong and Hainan; the central areas cover 6 provinces: Shanxi, Anhui, Jiangxi, Henan, Hubei and Hunan; the western areas include 12 provinces, autonomous regions and municipalities: Inner Mongolia, Guangxi, Chongqing, Sichuan, Guizhou, Yunnan, Tibet, Shaanxi, Gansu, Qinghai, Ningxia and Xinjiang; the northeastern areas include 3 provinces: Liaoning, Jilin and Heilongjiang.

44. Private investment in fixed assets refers to investment in the construction or purchase of fixed assets by domestic collective, private and individual-owned enterprises or organizations or their holding enterprises (with absolute holding and relative holding enterprises).

investment in fixed assets (excluding by rural households). The investment in infrastructure[45] saw an increase of 3.8 percent. The investment in the six major high energy consuming industries grew by 1.4 percent.

Figure 15: Shares of Investment in Fixed Assets of the Three Industries (Excluding by Rural Households) 2014-2018

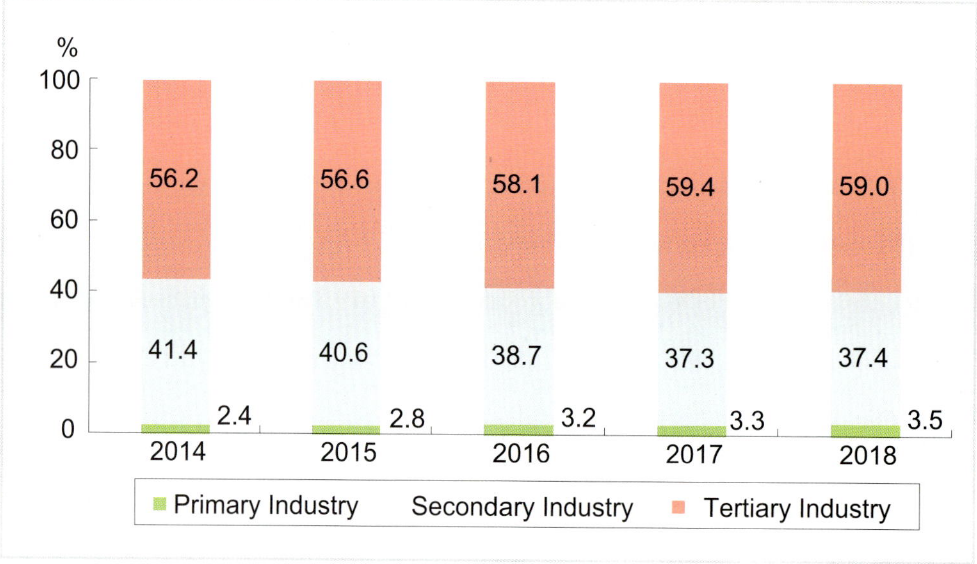

Table 6: Growth Rates of Investment in Fixed Assets (Excluding by Rural Households) by Sectors in 2018

Sector	Increase over 2017 (%)	Sector	Increase over 2017 (%)
Total	**5.9**	Financial Intermediation	-13.1
Agriculture, Forestry, Animal Husbandry and Fishery	12.3	Real Estate[46]	8.3
Mining	4.1	Leasing and Business Services	14.2
Manufacturing	9.5	Scientific Research and Technical Services	13.6
Production and Supply of Electricity, Heat, Gas and Water	-6.7	Water Conservancy, Environment and Public Facilities Management	3.3
Construction	-13.9	Services to Households, Repair and Other Services	-14.4
Wholesale and Retail Trades	-21.5	Education	7.2
Transport, Storage and Post	3.9	Health and Social Service	8.4
Hotels and Catering Services	-3.4	Culture, Sports and Entertainment	21.2
Information Transmission, Software and Information Technology Services	4.0	Public Management, Social Security and Social Organizations	-18.0

45. Investment in infrastructure includes transportation, postal service, telecommunication, radio, TV and satellite transmission, internet and related services, water conservancy, environment and public facilities management.

46. The investment in real estate includes the investment in real estate development, construction of buildings for own use, property management, intermediary services and other real estate investment.

Table 7: Newly Increased Production and Operation Capacity through Fixed Assets Investment in 2018

Item	Unit	Volume
Newly increased power transformer equipment with a capacity of over 220 kilovolts	10000 kilovolt-amperes	22082
New railways put into operation	kilometer	4683
Of which: high-speed railways[47]	kilometer	4100
Extended or new double-track railways put into operation	kilometer	4711
Electrified railways put into operation	kilometer	6474
Length of New and rebuilt highways	kilometer	356045
Of which: Expressways	kilometer	6063
New throughput capacity of berths for over 10,000-tonnage ships	10000 tons/year	26428
New civil transportation airports	-	6
New lines of optical-fiber cables	10000 km	578

In 2018, the investment in real estate development was 12,026.4 billion yuan, up by 9.5 percent. Of this total, the investment in residential buildings reached 8,519.2 billion yuan, an increase of 13.4 percent, that in office buildings was 599.6 billion yuan, down by 11.3 percent, and that in buildings for commercial business was 1,417.7 billion yuan, down by 9.4 percent.

In 2018, some 6.26 million housing units were started to be rebuilt in rundown urban areas nationwide. The number of housing units rebuilt in rundown areas was 5.11 million. In rural areas of China, among the poverty-stricken households that had their economic status registered at the local governments, and 1.57 million[48] of them had witnessed their dilapidate houses rebuilt and renovated in 2018.

47. High-speed railways refer to railways with a maximum operating speed of 200 km/h and above and railways with a maximum operating speed less than 200 km/h but only for high speed trains.

48. It refers to the number of dilapidated houses rebuilt belonging to the poverty-stricken households that had their economic status registered at the local governments by the end of December 2018 which was reported by all provinces (autonomous regions and municipalities).

Table 8: Main Indicators for Real Estate Development and Sales and Their Growth Rates in 2018

Item	Unit	Volume	Increase over 2017 (%)
Value of Investment	100 million RMB	120264	9.5
Of which: residential buildings	100 million RMB	85192	13.4
Floor space of buildings under construction	10,000 square meters	822300	5.2
Of which: residential buildings	10,000 square meters	569987	6.3
Floor space of buildings newly started	10,000 square meters	209342	17.2
Of which: residential buildings	10,000 square meters	153353	19.7
Floor space of buildings completed	10,000 square meters	93550	-7.8
Of which: residential buildings	10,000 square meters	66016	-8.1
Sales of commercialized buildings	10,000 square meters	171654	1.3
Of which: residential buildings	10,000 square meters	147929	2.2
Funds for investment this year	100 million RMB	165963	6.4
Of which: domestic loans	100 million RMB	24005	-4.9
individual mortgage	100 million RMB	23706	-0.8

VII. Foreign Economic Relations

The total value of imports and exports of goods in 2018 reached 30,505.0 billion yuan, up by 9.7 percent over the previous year. Of this total, the value of goods exported was 16,417.7 billion yuan, up by 7.1 percent; the value of goods imported was 14,087.4 billion yuan, up by 12.9 percent. The surplus of trade in goods reached 2,330.3 billion yuan, down by 521.7 billion yuan over the previous year. The total value of goods imported from and exported to countries along the Belt and Road[49] was 8,365.7 billion yuan, an increase of 13.3 percent over the previous year. Of the total, the value of goods exported was 4,647.8 billion yuan, an increase of 7.9 percent; that of goods imported was 3,717.9 billion yuan, an increase of 20.9 percent.

49. The Belt and Road refers to the Silk Road Economic Belt and the 21st Century Maritime Silk Road.

Figure 16: Imports and Exports of Goods 2014-2018

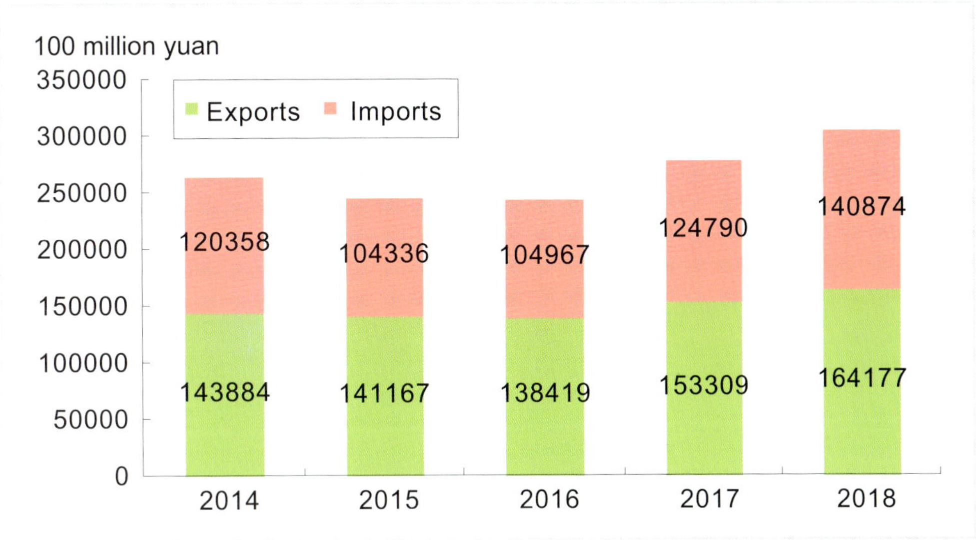

Table 9: Total Value of Import and Export of Goods and the Growth Rates in 2018

Item	Value (100 million yuan)	Increase over 2017 (%)
Total value of import and export of goods	**305050**	**9.7**
Exports	164177	7.1
Of which: General trade	92405	10.9
Processing trade	52676	2.5
Of which: Mechanical and electronic products	96457	7.9
High & new technology products	49374	9.3
Imports	140874	12.9
Of which: General trade	83947	14.3
Processing trade	31097	6.6
Of which: Mechanical and electronic products	63727	10.3
High & new technology products	44340	12.2
Trade surplus	**23303**	**-**

Table 10: Main Export Commodities in Volume and Value and the Growth Rates in 2018

Item	Unit	Volume	Increase over 2017 (%)	Value (100 million yuan)	Increase over 2017(%)
Rolled steel	10000 tons	6934	-8.1	3984	7.7
Textile yarns and textile articles	—	—	—	7851	5.1
Clothes and clothing accessories	—	—	—	10413	-2.3
Footwear	10000 tons	448	-0.4	3095	-5.4
Furniture and parts	—	—	—	3544	4.8
Luggage and similar containers	10000 tons	316	2.0	1787	-1.0
Toys	—	—	—	1662	2.3
Plastic articles	10000 tons	1312	12.3	2870	9.3
Integrated circuits	100 million pieces	2171	6.2	5591	23.5
Automatic data processing machines and components	10000 sets	147296	-4.4	11355	6.0
Handheld mobiles and car telephones	10000 sets	111918	-7.8	9343	9.8
Containers	10000 units	340	13.5	685	20.9
Liquid crystal display panels	10000 units	175810	-9.3	1527	-12.5
Motor vehicles	10000 sets	115	11.3	972	8.3

Table 11: Main Import Commodities in Volume and Value and the Growth Rates in 2018

Item	Unit	Volume	Increase over 2017 (%)	Value (100 million yuan)	Increase over 2017 (%)
Cereals and cereals flour	10000 tons	2047	-20.0	385	-12.4
Soybean	10000 tons	8803	-7.9	2502	-6.9
Edible vegetable oil	10000 tons	629	9.0	313	2.0
Iron ore and concentrate	10000 tons	106447	-1.0	4984	-4.0
Coal and lignite	10000 tons	28123	3.9	1613	4.9
Crude oil	10000 tons	46190	10.1	15882	43.1
Petroleum products refined	10000 tons	3348	13.0	1333	35.6
Natural gas	10000 tons	9039	31.9	2552	62.1
Plastics in primary forms	10000 tons	3284	14.5	3718	13.2
Paper pulp	10000 tons	2479	4.5	1300	25.1
Rolled steel	10000 tons	1317	-1.0	1083	5.5
Unwrought copper and its alloys	10000 tons	530	12.9	2469	16.5
Integrated circuits	100 million pieces	4176	10.8	20584	16.9
Motor vehicles	10000 sets	113	-8.5	3331	-2.7

Table 12: Imports and Exports of Goods by Major Countries and Regions, the Growth Rates and Proportions in 2018

Country or region	Exports (100 million yuan)	Increase over 2017 (%)	Proportion of the total (%)	Imports (100 million yuan)	Increase over 2017 (%)	Proportion of the total (%)
European Union	26974	7.0	16.4	18067	9.2	12.8
United States	31603	8.6	19.2	10195	-2.3	7.2
ASEAN	21066	11.3	12.8	17722	11.0	12.6
Japan	9709	4.4	5.9	11906	6.2	8.5
Republic of Korea	7174	3.1	4.4	13495	12.3	9.6
Hong Kong, China	19966	5.7	12.2	564	13.8	0.4
Taiwan, China	3212	7.9	2.0	11714	11.0	8.3
Brazil	2214	12.9	1.3	5119	28.2	3.6
Russia	3167	9.1	1.9	3909	39.4	2.8
India	5054	9.5	3.1	1242	12.2	0.9
South Africa	1072	6.9	0.7	1799	8.9	1.3

The total value of imports and exports of services[50] in 2018 was 5,240.2 billion yuan, up by 11.5 percent. The export value of services was 1,765.8 billion yuan, up by 14.6 percent. The import value of services was 3,474.4 billion yuan, up by 10.0 percent. The trade deficit in imports and exports of services was 1,708.6 billion yuan.

The year 2018 witnessed the establishment of 60,533 enterprises (excluding banking, securities and insurance) with foreign direct investment, up by 69.8 percent over the previous year, and the foreign direct investment actually utilized was 885.6 billion yuan , up by 0.9 percent, or 135.0 billion US dollars, up by 3.0 percent. Specifically, there were 4,479 newly established enterprises receiving direct investment from countries along the Belt and Road, up by 16.1 percent; and the foreign capital directly invested in China was 42.4 billion yuan, up by 13.2 percent, or 6.4 billion US dollars, up by 16.0 percent. In 2018, the foreign investment actually utilized by high technology manufacturing industry reached 89.8 billion yuan, up by 35.1 percent, or 13.7 billion US dollars, up by 38.1 percent.

50. The imports and exports of services are calculated according to the sixth edition of Balance of Payments and International Investment Position Manual (BPM6), and the growth rate is calculated on a comparable basis.

Table 13: Total Value of Foreign Direct Investment (Excluding Banking, Securities and Insurance) and the Growth Rates in 2018

Sector	Enterprises	Increase over 2017 (%)	Actually Utilized Value (100 million yuan)	Increase over 2017(%)
Total	**60533**	**69.8**	**8856**	**0.9**
Of which: Agriculture, Forestry, Animal Husbandry and Fishery	741	5.0	53	-26.4
Manufacturing	6152	23.4	2713	20.1
Production and Supply of Electricity, Heat, Gas and Water	284	-23.7	291	23.6
Transport, Storage and Post	754	45.8	314	-16.0
Information Transmission, Software and Information Technology	7222	127.9	773	-44.4
Wholesale and Retail Trades	22853	86.1	643	-16.5
Real Estate	1053	42.9	1489	31.4
Leasing and Business Services	9099	78.9	1196	6.4
Services to Households, Repair and Other Services	485	39.0	37	-2.6

In 2018, the non-financial outbound direct investment reached 797.4 billion yuan, down by 1.6 percent, or 120.5 billion US dollars, up by 0.3 percent, of this total, that to countries along the Belt and Road reached 15.6 billion US dollars, up by 8.9 percent.

Table 14: Total Value of Non-financial Outbound Direct Investment and the Growth Rates in 2018

Sector	Value (100 million US dollars)	Increase over 2017 (%)
Total	**1205**	**0.3**
Of which: Agriculture, Forestry, Animal Husbandry and Fishery	18	-20.3
Mining	92	11.3
Manufacturing	188	-1.6
Production and Supply of Electricity, Heat, Gas and Water	32	-0.9
Construction	74	0.8
Wholesale and Retail Trades	106	-57.5
Transport, Storage and Post Service	58	92.7
Information Transmission, Software and Information Technology	68	-33.7
Real Estate	40	82.0
Leasing and Business Services	446	27.6

In 2018, the accomplished business revenue through contracted overseas engineering projects was 1,118.6 billion yuan, down by 1.7 percent, or 169.0 billion US dollars, up by 0.3 percent. Specifically, the accomplished business revenue from countries along the Belt and Road was 89.3 billion US dollars, an increase of 4.4 percent, accounting for 52.8 percent of the accomplished business revenue through contracted overseas engineering projects. The number of labor forces sent abroad through overseas labor contracts was 490 thousand.

VIII. Finance and Financial Intermediation

The general public budget revenue reached 18,335.2 billion yuan in 2018, up by 6.2 percent, of which tax revenue amounted to 15,640.1 billion yuan, an increase of 1,203.1 billion yuan, up by 8.3 percent. The value of local government bonds issued to replace outstanding debt in 2018 reached 1,313.0 billion yuan, with an average interest rate of 3.89 percent. From 2015 to 2018, the bonds issued to replace outstanding debts totaled 12.2 trillion yuan, fulfilling the replacement goal set for existing government debt. Through replacement, the average interest rate of local government debt at the end of 2018 was 6.5 percentage points lower than that at the end of 2014, saving approximately 1.7 trillion yuan in interest payment.

Figure 17: General Public Budget Revenue 2014-2018

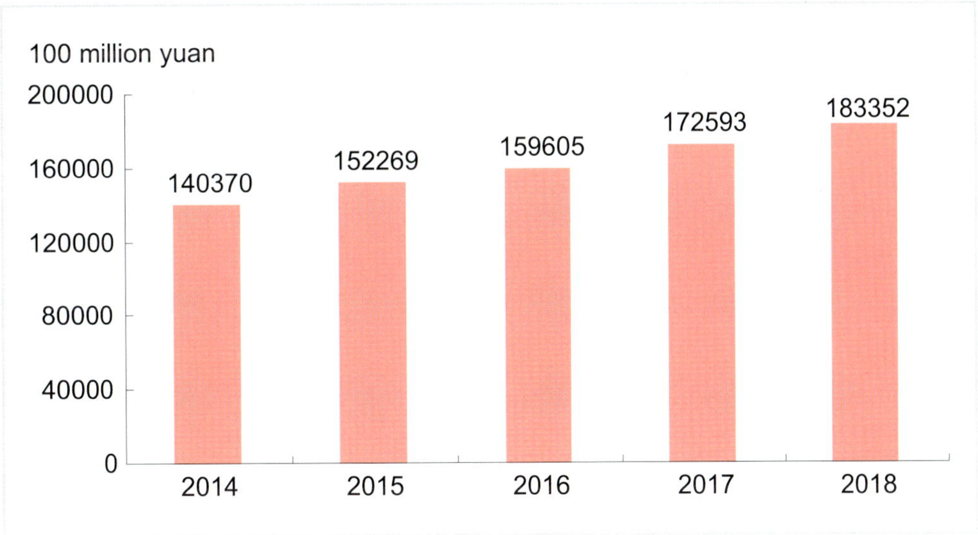

Note: Data for general public budget revenue from 2014 to 2017 as shown in the figure were final accounts and that of 2018 was the executive accounts.

By the end of 2018, money supply of broad sense (M_2) was 182.7 trillion yuan, an increase of 8.1 percent over that by the end of the previous year. Money supply of narrow sense (M_1) was 55.2 trillion yuan, up by 1.5 percent. Cash in circulation (M_0) was 7.3 trillion yuan, up by 3.6 percent.

In 2018, the increment of social financing[51] reached 19.3 trillion yuan, or 3.1 trillion yuan less than that in 2017 on a comparable basis. The balance of social financing[52] totaled 200.7 trillion yuan at the end of 2018, up by 9.8 percent compared with that at the end of 2017. Savings deposit in Renminbi and foreign currencies in all items of financial institutions totaled 182.5 trillion yuan at the end of 2018, an increase of 13.2 trillion yuan compared with that at the beginning of the year. Of this total, the savings deposit in Renminbi stood at 177.5 trillion yuan, an increase of 13.4 trillion yuan. Loans in Renminbi and foreign currencies in all items of financial institutions reached 141.8 trillion yuan, an increase of 16.2 trillion yuan. Of this total, loans in Renminbi were 136.3 trillion yuan, an increase of 16.2 trillion yuan.

Table 15: Savings Deposit and Loans in RMB and Foreign Currencies in All Financial Institutions and the Growth Rates at the End of 2018

Item	Year-end figure (100 million yuan)	Increase over 2017 (%)
Savings deposit	**1825158**	**7.8**
Domestic households	724439	11.1
Deposits in RMB	716038	11.2
Domestic non-financial enterprises	589105	3.1
Loans	**1417516**	**12.9**
Domestic short-term loans	443200	7.8
Domestic medium and long-term loans	854571	13.8

Loans in Renminbi from rural financial institutions (rural credit cooperatives, rural cooperation banks and rural commercial banks) totaled 16,982.2 billion yuan by the end of 2018, an increase of 2,000.2 billion yuan as compared with the beginning of the year. The loans in Renminbi for consumption use from all financial institutions totaled 37,790.3 billion yuan, an increase of 6,270.9 billion yuan. Of the total, short-term personal loans totaled 8,799.4 billion yuan, an increase of 1,998.9 billion yuan, and medium and long-term personal loans reached 28,990.9 billion yuan, an increase of 4,272.0 billion yuan.

Funds raised through domestic exchange markets[53] amounted to 6,436.5 billion yuan in 2018, an

51. The increment of social financing refers to the total funds raised by real economy from the financial system over a period of time.

52. The balance of social financing refers to the balance of the funds raised by real economy from the financial system at the end of a certain period of time (a month, a quarter or a year).

53. Funds raised through domestic stock markets are calculated by the money raised on the listing date.

increase of 1,357.2 billion yuan from the previous year. Of this total, 105 A-shares were newly issued, raising 137.8 billion yuan worth of capital altogether, down by 92.3 billion yuan. The refinancing of A-shares (including public newly issued, targeted placement, right issued, and preferred stock) raised 550.5 billion yuan, a decrease of 250.4 billion yuan. Various types of market entities financed 5,687.8 billion yuan through issuing bonds (including corporate bonds, convertible bonds, exchangeable bonds, financial bonds issued by policy banks, local government bonds and asset-backed securities) on Shanghai and Shenzhen Stock Exchanges, up by 1,773.1 billion yuan. In 2018, 577 companies were newly listed on National Equities Exchange and Quotations[54] and funds raised by listed companies reached 60.4 billion yuan.

In 2018, 7.79 trillion yuan corporate debenture bonds[55] were issued, an increase of 1.92 trillion yuan over the previous year.

The premium of primary insurance received by the insurance companies[56] totaled 3,801.7 billion yuan in 2018, up by 3.9 percent over that of the previous year. Of this total, life insurance premium of primary insurance amounted to 2,072.3 billion yuan, health and casualty insurance premium of primary insurance 652.4 billion yuan, and property insurance premium of primary insurance 1,077.0 billion yuan. Insurance companies paid an indemnity worth of 1,229.8 billion yuan, of which, life insurance indemnity was 438.9 billion yuan, health and casualty insurance indemnity 201.2 billion yuan, and property insurance indemnity 589.7 billion yuan.

IX. Households Income and Consumption and Social Security

In 2018, the per capita disposable income nationwide was 28,228 yuan, an increase of 8.7 percent or a real increase of 6.5 percent after deducting price factors. The median[57] of per capita disposable income nationwide was 24,336 yuan, up by 8.6 percent. In terms of usual residence, the per capita disposable income of urban households was 39,251 yuan, up by 7.8 percent over that of 2017, or a real growth of 5.6 percent after deducting price factors. The median of per capita disposable income of urban households was 36,413 yuan, up by 7.6 percent. The per capita disposable income of rural households was 14,617 yuan, up by 8.8

54. National Equities Exchange and Quotations, also called "the New Over-the-Counter Market", is a national securities exchange established upon approval by the State Council in 2012. Preferred stocks were excluded from Funds raised by listed companies in National Equities Exchange and Quotations.

55. Corporate debenture bonds include debt financing instruments of non-financial businesses, enterprise bonds, corporate bonds and convertible bonds.

56. The premium of primary insurance received by the insurance companies refers to the premium income from primary insurance contracts confirmed by the insurance companies.

57. The median of per capita income refers to the per capita income of household lied in the middle of all surveyed households which are ranked from low to high (or high to low) based on per capita income level.

percent, or 6.6 percent in real terms. The median of per capita disposable income of rural households was 13,066 yuan, up by 9.2 percent. Grouped by income quintile[58], the per capita disposable income of low-income group reached 6,440 yuan, the lower-middle-income group 14,361 yuan, the middle-income group 23,189 yuan, the upper-middle-income group 36,471 yuan and the high-income group 70,640 yuan. The per capita monthly income of migrant workers was 3,721 yuan, increased by 6.8 percent over the previous year.

The national per capita consumption expenditure was 19,853 yuan, up by 8.4 percent, or a real growth of 6.2 percent after deducting price factors. In terms of usual residence, the per capita consumption expenditure of urban households was 26,112 yuan, up by 6.8 percent, or 4.6 percent in real terms after deducting price factors. The per capita consumption expenditure of rural households was 12,124 yuan, up by 10.7 percent, or a real growth of 8.4 percent after deducting price factors. The national Engel's Coefficient stood at 28.4 percent, 0.9 percentage point lower than that of the previous year, with that of urban and rural households standing at 27.7 percent and 30.1 percent respectively.

Figure 18: National Per Capita Disposable Income and its Growth Rates 2014-2018

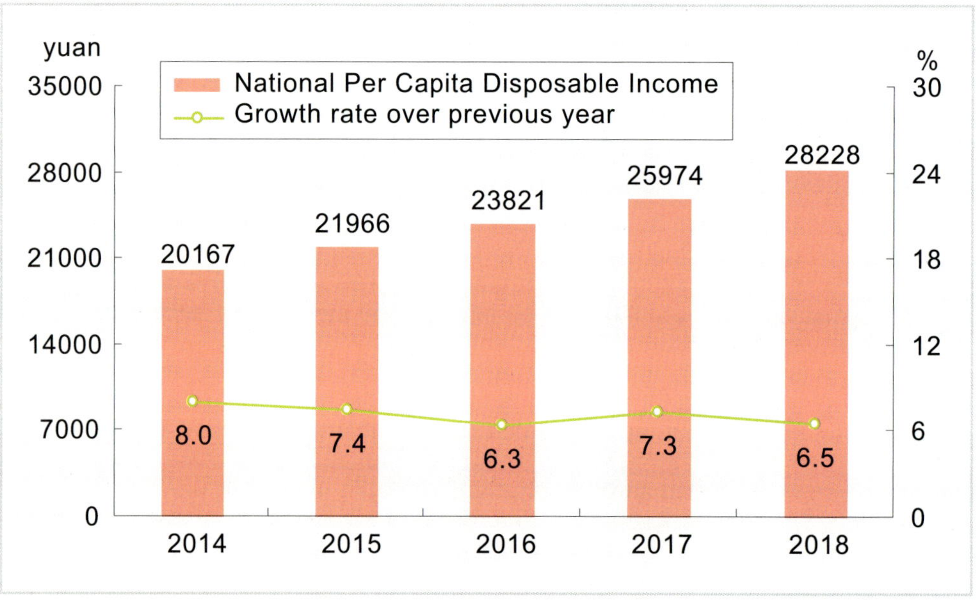

58. The income quintile refers to the five equal partitions of all surveyed households, who are ranked from low to high based on per capita income level. The top 20 percent with the highest income are classified as high-income group, and the other four levels are upper-middle-income group, middle-income group, lower-middle-income group and low-income group.

Figure 19: National Per Capita Consumption Expenditure and Composition in 2018

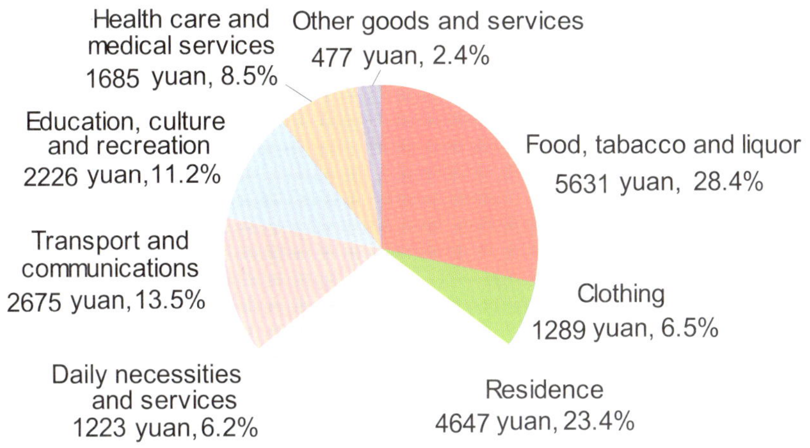

By the end of 2018, a total of 418.48 million people participated in urban basic pension program for staff and workers, a year-on-year increase of 15.55 million. A total of 523.92 million people participated in basic pension insurance program for urban and rural residents, an increase of 11.37 million. A total of 1,344.52 million people participated in basic medical insurance program, an increase of 167.71 million. Of this total, 316.73 million people participated in the program for staff and workers, an increase of 13.51 million, and 897.41 million people participated in the program for urban and rural residents, an increase of 23.82 million. Some 196.43 million people participated in unemployment insurance program, an increase of 8.59 million. The number of people receiving unemployment insurance payment stood at 2.23 million by the end of 2018. A total of 238.68 million people participated in work accident insurance, an increase of 11.45 million, of which 80.85 million were migrant workers, an increase of 2.78 million. A total of 204.35 million people participated in maternity insurance programs, an increase of 11.35 million. Minimum living allowances were granted to 10.08 million urban residents and 35.20 million rural residents, and 4.55 million rural residents living in extreme poverty[59] received relief and assistance and 10.75 million person-times received temporary assistance[60]. A total of 49.72 million people were financed to participate in basic medical insurance program

59. Rural residents living in extreme poverty refer to the aged, the disabled and the minor under 16 years of age in rural areas who have no ability to work, no sources of income and no statutory obligors to provide for them, bring them up or support them, or whose statutory obligors have no ability to fulfill their obligations.

60. Temporary assistance refers to emergent and transitional assistance the government provides to families or individuals who experience hardships because of emergencies, unexpected harm, major diseases or other unusual factors and are not covered by other forms of social assistance programs or still suffer hardships after receiving other social assistance programs.

and medical assistance was granted to 38.25 million person-times. National subsidies and allowances were provided to 8.61 million veterans and other entitled people.

By the end of 2018, there were altogether 33 thousand social welfare institutions providing accommodation, of which 30 thousand were elder-caring organizations and 664 were children caring organizations. The social welfare institutions provided 7.824 million beds[61], of which 7.463 million were for the elderly and 104 thousand were for children. By the end of 2018, there were 27 thousand community service centers and 145 thousand community service stations.

X. Science & Technology and Education

Expenditures on research and experimental development activities (R&D) were worth 1,965.7 billion yuan in 2018, up by 11.6 percent over 2017, accounting for 2.18 percent of GDP. Of this total, 111.8 billion yuan was appropriated for basic research programs. A total number of 1,052 projects were arranged under the national key research and development program. Another 563 subject researches were arranged under the national science and technology major projects and 44,504 projects were financed by the National Natural Science Foundation. By the end of 2018, there were altogether 501 state key laboratories in operation, 132 national engineering research centers, 217 national engineering laboratories, and 1,480 national enterprise technical centers. The National Fund for Technology Transfer and Commercialization established 21 sub-funds, with the total size reaching 31.3 billion yuan. There were 4,323 thousand patent applications from home and abroad, up by 16.9 percent, and a total of 2,447 thousand were authorized, up by 33.3 percent. The number of PCT patent applications accepted[62] was 55 thousand. By the end of 2018, the number of patents in force was 8.381 million, of which 1,602 thousand were invention patents from home. The number of invention patents per 10,000 people was 11.5. A total of 412 thousand technology transfer contracts were signed, representing 1,769.7 billion yuan in value, up by 31.8 percent over the previous year.

61. The beds provided by social welfare institutions include those provided by adoption agencies, aid agencies, community agencies, serviceman recreation habitation and military supply stations etc.

62. The number of PCT patent applications accepted refers to the number of PCT patent application accepted by the State Intellectual Property Office which acts as the receiving office of PCT patent application. PCT is the abbreviation of Patent Cooperation Treaty, which is a treaty for international cooperation in the field of patents.

Figure 20: The Amount of Expenditure on Research and Experimental Development Activities (R&D) and its Growth Rates 2014-2018

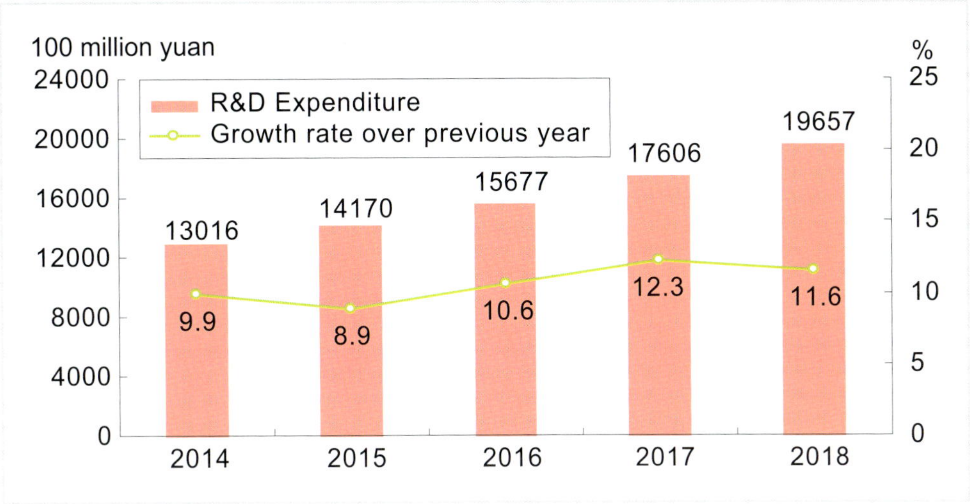

Table 16: Number of Patent Applications, Patents Authorized and Patents in Force in 2018

Item	Patents (10,000)	Increase over 2017 (%)
Number of patent applications	**432.3**	**16.9**
Of which: domestic	412.1	17.3
Of which: for new inventions	154.2	11.6
Of which: domestic	138.1	11.9
Number of patents authorized	**244.7**	**33.3**
Of which: domestic	231.9	36.0
Of which: for new inventions	43.2	2.9
Of which: domestic	34.0	6.0
Number of patents in force at the end of the year	**838.1**	**17.3**
Of which: domestic	739.9	19.3
Of which: for new inventions	236.6	13.5
Of which: domestic	160.2	18.1

The year 2018 saw 38 times of successful satellite launches. Chang'e-4 probe made a successful landing on the far side of the moon and transmitted data back to the earth via the relay satellite, marking the beginning of exploration on the far side of the moon for the first time in human history. The basic system for Beidou-3 was completed, providing global services. The China-Italy Electromagnetic Monitoring Experiment

Satellite by the first space-based platform for China′s stereo seismic monitoring system and the first China-France Oceanography satellite under Sino-French space cooperation were launched successfully. The second aircraft carrier started its sea trial, the domestically-made amphibious aircraft completed maiden water takeoff and the Hongkong-Zhuhai-Macao Bridge officially opened to the traffic.

By the end of 2018, there were altogether 791 national quality inspection centers. There were 484 agencies for product quality and management system and service certification, accumulatively 630,000 enterprises were certified. There were 5,030 authorized measurement institutions in the year, enforcing compulsory inspection on 104.06 million measurement instruments. A total of 2,668 national standards were developed or revised in the year, including 1,935 new standards. The qualification rate of manufactured products[63] reached 93.93 percent.

In 2018, the post-graduate education enrollment was 2.731 million students with 858 thousand new students and 604 thousand graduates. The general tertiary education enrollment was 28.310 million students with 7.910 million new students and 7.533 million graduates. Vocational secondary schools[64] had 15.552 million enrolled students, including 5.570 million new entrants, and 4.873 million graduates. Senior secondary schools had 23.754 million enrolled students, including 7.927 million new entrants, and 7.792 million graduates. Students enrolled in junior secondary schools totaled 46.526 million, including 16.026 million new entrants, and 13.678 million graduates. The country had a primary education enrollment of 103.393 million students, including 18.673 million new entrants, and 16.165 million graduates. There were 666 thousand students enrolled in special education schools, with 124 thousand new entrants and 81 thousand graduates. Kindergartens accommodated 46.564 million children. The number of students graduating from compulsory education reached 94.2 percent of the total enrollment, the gross enrollment rate in senior high schools reached 88.8 percent.

63. The qualification rate of manufactured products is the ratio of the samples that have passed the sampling quality test, the process of which follows certain methods, procedure and standard, to the total amount of the sampled products. The survey samples cover 29 sectors of the manufacturing industry.

64. Vocational secondary schools include regular specialized secondary schools, adult specialized secondary schools, vocational high schools and skilled workers schools.

Figure 21: Enrollment in Education 2014-2018

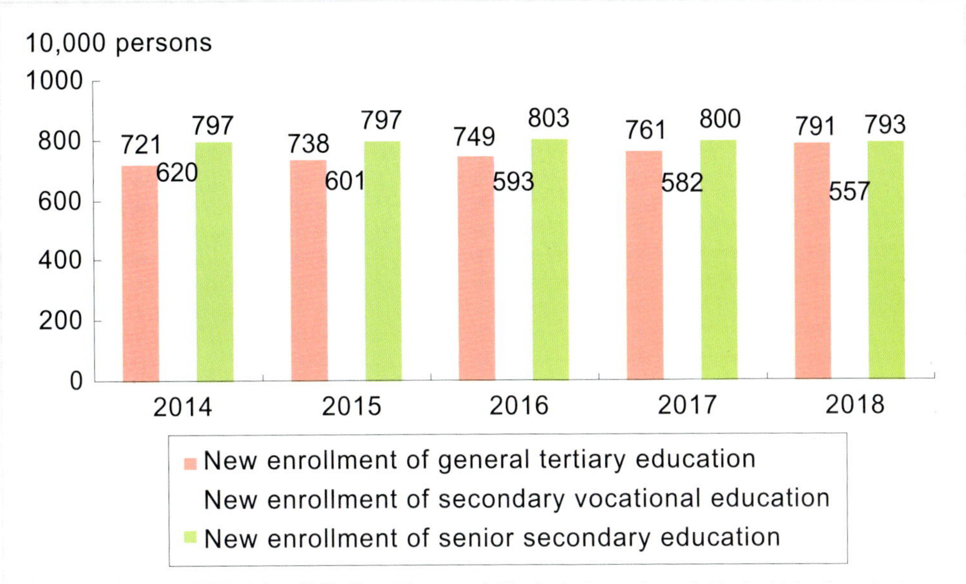

XI. Culture and Tourism, Public Health and Sports

At the end of 2018, there were 2,075 art-performing groups and 3,331 museums in the cultural system throughout China. A total of 3,173 public libraries received[65] 845.29 million people. There were 3,326 cultural centers. Subscribers to cable television programs numbered 214 million, in which 202 million subscribed to digital cable television programs. Radio broadcasting and television broadcasting coverage rates were 98.9 percent and 99.3 percent respectively. A total of 13,726 episodes of 323 TV series and 86,257 minutes of TV cartoons were made in 2018. The country produced 902 feature movies and 180 science, educational, documentary, cartoon and special movies[66]. A total of 34.0 billion copies of newspapers and 2.4 billion copies of magazines were issued, and 9.5 billion copies of books were published. The average number of books possessed per person[67] was 6.85 copies. By the end of the year, there were 4,210 archives in China and 140.16 million files were made accessible to the public.

The year 2018 registered 5.54 billion domestic tourists, up by 10.8 percent over the previous year. The revenue from domestic tourism totaled 5,127.8 billion yuan, up by 12.3 percent. The number of inbound

65. People received by the public libraries refer to the number of people who visit libraries and use library services in the year, including borrowing and reading books, consultation and attending readers' programs.

66. Special movies refers to those using different display modes in terms of projection techniques, equipment and program as compared with the ordinary cinemas, such as IMAX movies, 3D movies, 4D movies, multidimensional movies and full dome movies.

67. The average number of books possessed per person refers to the average number of books published in the year that can be possessed per person in China.

visitors to China totaled 141.20 million, an increase of 1.2 percent. Of this total, 30.54 million were foreigners, up by 4.7 percent; and 110.66 million were Chinese compatriots from Hong Kong, Macao and Taiwan, up by 0.3 percent. Of all the inbound tourists, overnight visitors counted 62.90 million, an increase of 3.6 percent. Earnings from international tourism topped 127.1 billion US dollars, up by 3.0 percent. The number of China's outbound visitors totaled 161.99 million, up by 13.5 percent. Of this total, 155.02 million were on private visits, an increase of 14.1 percent; and 99.19 million visited Hong Kong, Macao and Taiwan, up by 14.0 percent.

Figure 22: The Person-times of Domestic Tourists and its Growth Rates 2014-2018

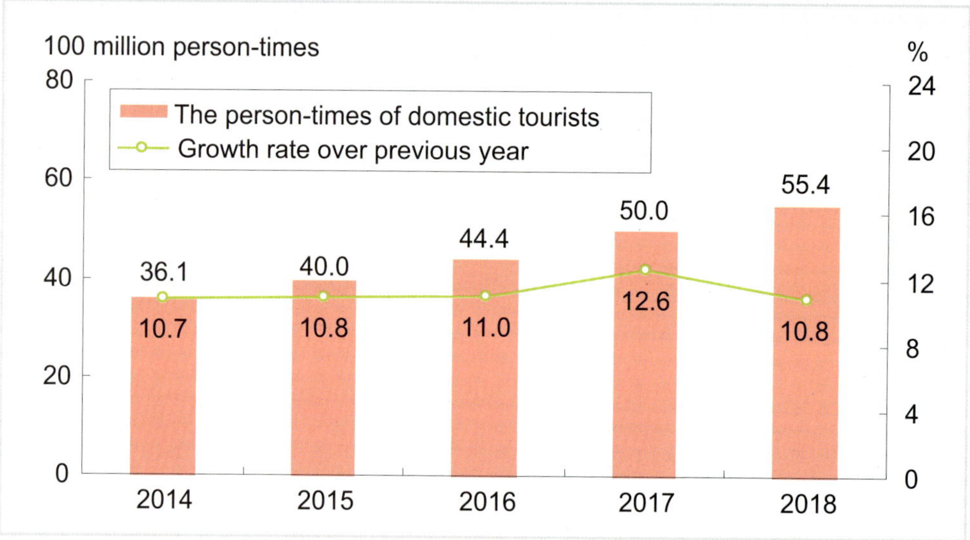

By the end of 2018, there were 1,004,000 medical and health institutions in China, including 32,000 hospitals. Of all the hospitals, 12,000 were public, and 20,000 were private. Of the 950,000 medical and health institutions at grass-root level, there were 36,000 township health centers, 35,000 community health service centers, 248,000 clinics and 630,000 village clinics. Of the 19,000 professional public health institutions, 3,469 were disease control and prevention centers and 3,141 were health monitoring institutions. By the end of 2018, there were 9.50 million medical technical personnel in China, including 3.58 million licensed doctors and licensed assistant doctors and 4.12 million registered nurses. The medical and health institutions in China possessed 8.45 million beds, of which, hospitals possessed 6.56 million and township health centers had 1.34 million. The total number of medical visits[68] and hospital discharges[69] in 2018 reached 8.42 billion and 260 million respectively.

Figure 23: Year-end Number of Medical Technical Personnel 2014-2018

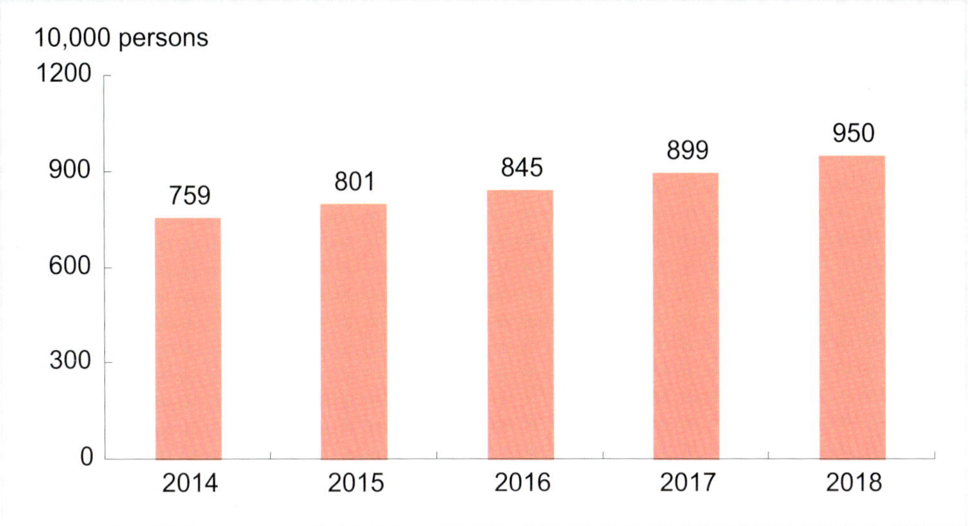

In 2018, Chinese athletes won 118 world championships on 24 sports events and broke 15 world records. Chinese physically-challenged athletes won 50 world championships in 20 international sports competitions.

XII. Resources, Environment and Emergency Management

In 2018, the total supply of state-owned land for construction use[70] was 643 thousand hectares, an increase of 6.6 percent over the previous year. Of this total, the supply for mining storage was 132 thousand hectares, up by 7.2 percent; that for real estate[71] was 144 thousand hectares, up by 24.6 percent; and that for infrastructure facilities was 368 thousand hectares, up by 0.7 percent.

The total stock of water resources in 2018 was 2,796.0 billion cubic meters. With an increase of

68. The total number of medical visits refers to the number of people receiving medical services, including outpatient services, emergency treatment, home visits, appointment-based diagnosis and treatment, health check-up of a specific item, and health consultation and guidance (excluding health lectures).

69. The number of hospital discharges refers to the number of inpatients discharged from hospitals in the reporting period, including those who are discharged from hospitals or transferred to other medical institutions following doctors' advice, discharged from hospitals without doctors' permission, dead or other situations. The number of people who are recovered from family sickbeds is excluded.

70. Total supply of state-owned land for construction use refers to the supply of state-owned land for construction use with the land-used right sold, allocated or leased to units or individuals by the municipal or county governments according to annual land supply plan and in line with relevant laws in the reporting period.

71. Land used for real estate refers to the sum of land used for commercial service and for residence.

1.1 percent over 2017, the total water consumption reached 611.0 billion cubic meters, of which water consumption for living purposes rose by 1.4 percent, for industrial use grew by 0.6 percent, for agricultural use up by 1.1 percent, and for ecological water supplement grew by 3.8 percent. Water consumption for every 10 thousand yuan worth of GDP produced[72] was 73 cubic meters, a decline of 5.1 percent over the previous year. Water consumption for every 10 thousand yuan worth of industrial value added was 45 cubic meters, down by 5.2 percent. Per capita water consumption was 439 cubic meters, up by 0.6 percent.

In 2018, the total area of afforestation reached 7.07 million hectares, of which 3.60 million hectares were afforested by manpower, accounting for 50.9 percent of the total. Forest tending areas reached 8.52 million hectares. By the end of 2018, there were 474 national natural reserves. A total of 54 thousand square kilometers of eroded land was put under treatment programs.

Preliminary estimation indicated that the total energy consumption in 2018 amounted to 4.64 billion tons of standard coal equivalent, up by 3.3 percent over 2017. The consumption of coal increased by 1.0 percent; crude oil, up by 6.5 percent; natural gas, up by 17.7 percent; and electric power, up by 8.5 percent. The consumption of coal accounted for 59.0 percent of the total energy consumption, 1.4 percentage points lower than that of 2017, while clean energy consumption, such as natural gas, hydropower, nuclear power and wind power accounted for 22.1 percent, 1.3 percentage points higher. The comprehensive energy consumption per unit caustic soda of key energy-intensive industrial enterprises went down by 0.5 percent, per unit synthetic ammonia down by 0.7 percent, per ton steel down by 3.3 percent and per unit copper smelting down by 4.7 percent. The standard coal consumption per kilowatt-hour of thermal power generation was decreased by 0.7 percent. The carbon dioxide emission per 10,000 yuan worth of GDP was cut by 4.0 percent.

72. The consumption of water for producing 10 thousand yuan worth of GDP and 10 thousand yuan worth of industrial value added are calculated at 2015 constant prices.

Figure 24: The Proportion of Clean Energy Consumption in the Total Energy Consumption 2014-2018

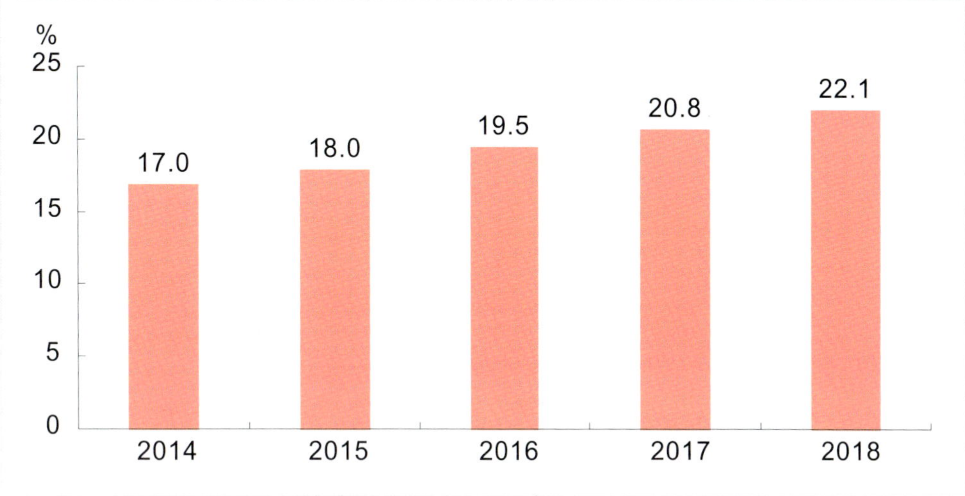

Monitoring of oceanic water quality at 417 offshore monitoring stations indicated that oceanic water met the national quality standard Grade I and II at 74.6 percent of the stations; water quality at 6.7 percent of the stations met Grade III standard; and water of Grade IV or inferior quality was found at 18.7 percent of the stations.

Of the monitored 338 cities at prefecture level and above, 35.8 percent reached the air standard and 64.2 percent failed. The annual average concentration of particulate matter ($PM_{2.5}$) for cities (based on 262 cities failed to reach the standard of annual average concentration in 2015) that failed to meet the standard stood at 43 micrograms per cubic meter, down by 10.4 percent over the previous year.

Of the 323 cities subject to noise monitoring program, 4.0 percent enjoyed fairly good environment, 63.5 percent had good environment, 30.7 percent had fair environment, 1.2 percent had poor environment and 0.6 percent had very poor environment in downtown areas.

The average temperature in 2018 was 10.09 ℃ , down by 0.30 ℃ compared with that of the previous year. Typhoons hit China 10 times in 2018.

In 2018, natural disasters hit 20.81 million hectares of crops, of which 2.59 million hectares of crops were demolished. Flood, waterlogging and geological disasters caused a direct economic loss of 106.1 billion yuan. Droughts caused a direct economic loss of 25.5 billion yuan. Disasters from low temperature, frost and snow made a total direct economic loss of 43.4 billion yuan. Oceanic disasters caused a direct economic loss of 4.8 billion yuan. The country recorded 16 earthquakes with magnitude 5 and over, 11 of which caused disasters, causing a direct economic loss of 3.0 billion yuan. The year 2018 witnessed 2,478 forest fires, with

16 thousand hectares of forests damaged.

The death toll due to work accidents amounted to 34,046 people. Work accidents in industrial, mining and commercial enterprises caused 1.547 deaths out of every 100 thousand employees, down by 5.6 percent over 2017. The death toll for one million tons of coal produced in coalmines was 0.093 people, down by 12.3 percent. The road traffic death toll per 10 thousand vehicles was 1.93 people, down by 6.3 percent.

Data Sources:

In this Communiqué, data of urbanization rate of population with household registration, motor vehicles for civilian use and traffic accidents are from the Ministry of Public Security; data of newly increased employed people in urban areas, registered unemployment rate, social security and skilled workers schools are from the Ministry of Human Resources and Social Security; data of foreign exchange reserves and exchange rate are from the State Administration of Foreign Exchange; data of output of aquatic products are from Ministry of Agriculture and Rural Affairs; data of production of timber, area of afforestation, forest tending areas, national natural reserves are from the National Forestry and Grassland Administration; data of areas with effective irrigation system, water resources and soil erosion are from the Ministry of Water Resources; data of installed power generation capacity and newly increased power transformer equipment with a capacity of over 220 kilovolts and above are from the China Electricity Council; data of volume of freight handled by ports, container shipping of ports, highway transportation, waterway transportation, new and rebuilt highways, new throughput capacity of berths for over 10,000-tonnage ships are from the Ministry of Transport; data of railway transportation, new railways put into operation, new double-track railways put into operation and electrified railways put into operation are from China Railway; data of civil aviation and new civil transportation airports are from the Civil Aviation Administration of China; data of pipelines are from China National Petroleum Corporation, China Petrochemical Corporation and China National Offshore Oil Corporation; data of postal service are from State Post Bureau; data of telecommunication, software revenue, and new lines of optical-fiber cables are from the Ministry of Industry and Information Technology; data of housing units rebuilt in rundown areas and dilapidated houses rebuilt belonging to poor rural households that had their economic status registered at local governments are from the Ministry of Housing and Urban-Rural Development; data of imports and exports of goods are from the General Administration of Customs; data of imports and exports of services, foreign direct investment, outbound direct investment, overseas contracted projects and overseas labor contracts are from the Ministry of Commerce; data of finance are from the Ministry of Finance; data of monetary finance and corporate debenture bonds are from the People's Bank of China; data of funds raised through domestic exchange markets are from China Securities Regulatory Commission; data of the insurance sector are from China Banking and Insurance Regulatory Commission; data of medical insurance, people financed to participate in basic medical insurance program and medical assistance are from the National Healthcare and Security Administration; data of urban and rural minimum living allowances, relief and assistance granted to rural residents living in extreme poverty, temporary assistance and social services are from the Ministry of Civil Affairs; data of entitled people are from the Ministry of Veterans Affairs; data of national key research and experimental development programs, national science and technology major projects, state key laboratories, National Fund for Technology Transfer and Commercialization and technology transfer contracts are from the Ministry of Science and Technology; data of natural science foundation projects are from the National Natural Science Foundation; data of national engineering research centers, national engineering laboratories and enterprise technical centers are from the National Development and Reform Commission; data of patents are from the National Intellectual Property Administration; data of satellite launches are from the State Administration of Science, Technology and Industry for National Defense; data of quality inspection, national standards developed or revised and the qualification rate of manufactured products are from the State Administration for Market Regulation; data of education are from the Ministry of Education; data of art-performing groups, museums, public libraries, cultural centers, books and tourism are from the Ministry of Culture and Tourism; data of television and radio programs are from the National Radio and Television Administration; data of movies are from the China Film Administration; data of newspapers and magazines are from the National Press and Publication Administration; data of files are from the State Archives Administration; data of outbound visitors are from the National Immigration Administration; data of medical care and health are from the National Health Commission; data of sports are from the General Administration of Sport; data of physically-challenged athletes are from the China Disabled Persons' Federation; data of supply of state-owned land for construction use and direct economic loss caused by oceanic disasters are from the Ministry of Natural Resources; data of the carbon dioxide emission per 10,000 yuan worth of GDP and environment monitoring are from the Ministry of Ecology and Environment; data of average temperature and typhoons are from the China Meteorological Administration; data of areas of crops hit by natural disasters, direct economic loss caused by flood, waterlogging and geological disasters, direct economic loss caused by droughts, direct economic loss caused by low temperature, frost and snow, forest fires, areas of forests damaged and work safety are from the Ministry of Emergency Management; data of the number of earthquakes and direct economic loss caused by earthquakes are from the China Earthquake Administration; all the other data are from the National Bureau of Statistics.

In case of any differences between English translation and the original Chinese text, the Chinese edition shall prevail.